T0209150

GOLF

**AMONG THE VEGETABLES
AND THE
SEVEN-CLUB CHALLENGE**

GOLF

AMONG THE VEGETABLES
AND THE
SEVEN-CLUB CHALLENGE

JOHN B. NANNINGA

⊂iUniverse®

GOLF AMONG THE VEGETABLES AND THE SEVEN-CLUB CHALLENGE

iUniverse books may be ordered through booksellers or by contacting:

iUniverse
1663 Liberty Drive
Bloomington, IN 47403
www.iuniverse.com
844-349-9409

ISBN: 978-1-6632-5744-4 (sc)
ISBN: 978-1-6632-5746-8 (hc)
ISBN: 978-1-6632-5745-1 (e)

Library of Congress Control Number: 2023920619

Print information available on the last page.

iUniverse rev. date: 01/12/2024

CHAPTER 1

A course that continually offers problems, one with fight in it, if
you please, is the one that keeps the player keen for the game.
—Donald J. Ross

Yet not only is every golf pitch different from all others,
but it consists of little pitches within itself. Thus, an almost
inexhaustible supply of golfing problems presents itself.
—Henry Longhurst, golf writer

The invitation arrived at the end of March. I had returned home from my
post at the United Sports Agency and found a letter on my desk, bearing
a British Air Mail stamp. Upon opening the letter, I found it was from
my friend and fellow sportswriter in England, Dick Whistle, who had
obtained an invitation for me to attend a unique golf tournament in which
a sportswriter and a professional golfer compete as a team. The format
is alternate shot (foursomes). The competition is held on a links located
on a former vegetable farm at Gnomewood-by-Sea, in England, and each
player may use only seven clubs.

The tournament was initiated by Sir Harold Gilroy before World War
II and resumed after hostilities had ceased and repairs to the course had
been completed. It initially acquired the title "Pros, Poets, and the Seven
Club Challenge." Dick added in the invitation that he would be playing in
the tournament. Naturally, I responded, turning to my Underwood and
typing a reply that I would be delighted to attend.

I had known Dick, dating back to World War II, when we were war
correspondents for our respective countries. Before the war, he had been a
sportswriter for the *London Sports Reporter*, and I had been a sportswriter

for an upstate New York newspaper. During the war, our paths crossed on several occasions, and during a discussion on golf, Dick mentioned Sir Harold's tournament and its unique character. At the time, I recalled expressing interest in attending such a golf event sometime in the future. Now I would have that opportunity.

Consequently, in the last week of June, I boarded a flight to London where I would meet Dick, and we would travel by train to Gnomewood-by-Sea. While on the flight, I speculated how I might compete in such a tournament. Probably, the Bing Crosby golf tournament played at Pebble Beach is the closest to what I would imagine is played at Gnomewood. But in the Crosby tournament, the teams are composed of golf professionals and celebrities from the entertainment industry, professional and amateur sports, and CEOs from various corporations. The scoring is best ball; that is, a player's lowest score for that hole is counted. A nonprofessional may use their handicap if that will lower the team's score. In Sir Harold's tournament, according to Dick, a writer most have a handicap of fourteen or lower to compete, but their handicap is not used in the scoring. And a player may use only seven clubs rather than the fourteen that the rules allow. So, I concluded the Gnomewood tournament was unique. I couldn't help but reflect on how my fellow sportswriters might fare in such a tournament.

Arriving in London the next morning, I took a cab to Paddington train station and met Dick and several other sportswriters who were also departing for Gnomewood. Dick looked much the same since I had last seen him at Carnoustie in 1953. He now wore glasses to read and, along with graying hair, he had a serious, professorial look that belied his keen sense of humor. We boarded the train, and, as it departed, out came cigarettes, pipes, and an occasional flask.

On the trip, Dick elaborated on the history of the Gnomewood tournament. Sir Harold Gilroy, a wealthy newspaper and magazine publisher, believed some sportswriters were overly critical of the play of professionals in tournament competitions. He recognized that not every shot was easy, even though the player's swing might appear faultless. The weather, course conditions, especially the greens, and the presence of spectators could play a role in how a professional might score on a particular day. Consequently, Sir Harold initiated a tournament in which sportswriters and professionals would compete as teams in an alternate shot format (often referred to as foursomes). To induce professionals to compete, a cash prize was awarded to the winning pro on a team.

Sir Harold had staged the tournament twice before the war, and it was a modest success. One noncompeting sportswriter wrote, "The golf tournament organized by Sir Harold Gilroy was an entertaining display of combining the golfing abilities of golf writers and golf professionals." The members of the winning team were the pro Hylton Barleycroft and Belden Stratford, a sportswriter from Brighton, who played to a seven handicap. Barleycroft was injured in the war and subsequently confined his golf activities to teaching. His brother Byford, also a golf pro, has competed in the Gnomewood tournament in recent years, although he has yet to be on a winning team.

The tournament is played on a course located outside the village of Gnomewood-by-Sea and is known as Gnomewood Links. The links land on which the course was originally constructed had once been forest land, but erosion from the sea led to the trees giving way to sandy soil and arable land on which vegetables could be grown. The name, Gnomewood, is thought to have been derived from the time when trees were still visible from the sea, and at twilight, passing fishermen thought they could see small gnomelike figures dancing among the trees. The small fishing village located near the shoreline acquired the name Gnomewood-by-Sea sometime in the eighteenth century.

In the 1890s, the owner of property along the shoreline constructed a nine-hole golf course among vegetable-growing areas and established Gnomewood Links. It became popular enough so that, in the early twentieth century, a second nine holes were added, while still maintaining the vegetable-growing sites. A clubhouse was constructed about this time, and a six-bedroom mansion was built for the owner, which acquired the name Excelsior House. Sir Harold and his wife, Dorothy, occupy the mansion when they are not in their London home.

Two years after the war, Sir Harold resumed the tournament, having repaired several areas on the links where there was damage caused by German bombs. A V-1 flying bomb had crashed along the shoreline near the links, but it had failed to explode. To this day, it remains embedded in the sand. The clubhouse suffered minor damage from German fighter planes strafing it, presuming it was a radar site.

Following the war, some areas on the links that were devoted to growing vegetables to meet the needs of the civilian population were returned to fairways. By 1948, Sir Harold determined the course was ready for play. Professionals were regaining their prewar form, and sportswriters were returning to playing golf, a few taking up the game for the first time. Sir Harold now requires that writers invited to compete should have a handicap of fourteen or better.

Another unique feature of the tournament is the rule that only seven clubs may be used. Sir Harold believed this would even the competition between the pros and the sportswriter teams. The pros would have to decide which seven clubs offered the best opportunity for scoring. This would emphasize the ability to execute half and three-quarter shots. Over the years of watching and playing with amateurs, Sir Harold observed most amateurs were only proficient with six or seven clubs. The professionals invited were, for the most part, from Great Britain and Ireland, and they were used to playing in less than favorable weather conditions. Hopefully, this ability will be passed on to their sportswriter partners during the tournament.

The maintenance of Gnomewood Links is provided by a character known as old Leffingwell and his assistant, Grafton. Additional course work is provided by greenskeepers from nearby golf courses at Hidden Springs and Lydston Heath. The vegetables are grown by workers from Gnomewood. The clubhouse management is provided by Soufflé, a former member of the French underground during the war, who was retrieved by air, along with a British agent, shortly before the Normandy invasion. Soufflé is also a part-time chef at Excelsior House.

At this point in Dick's discourse about Gnomewood, the train began to slow down, indicating we were nearing our destination.

CHAPTER 2

The train pulled into Gnomewood-by-Sea station nearly on time. I noted the service on British Rail has improved since my previous visits to cover the Open. Accompanying Dick and me on the train were Arthur Mountebank, Fowler Thistletoe, and Bob Paltry. Fowler and Bob had competed previously in the Gnomewood Seven-Club Challenge and were looking forward to playing this year. Also in the group on the train were several young reporters, whom I looked forward to getting to know during the tournament.

As we left the train and picked up our luggage, we faced a pub, the Rake & Dibble, across the street. The younger writers suggested we enjoy a quick pint before departing for our hotel. They weren't sure of the availability of food and drink at Gnomewood Links, but Dick assured the group there would be no difficulty in replenishing our thirst when we arrived at the links. A small bus was waiting at the station to take us to our hotel, the Prince Rupert, where the sportswriters who had been invited to attend the tournament were staying, and then on to the Foggy Shores Hotel, where the professionals, caddies, and a few writers not previously invited were staying.

The Prince Rupert was an old half-timbered structure with exposed wooden beams inside, some of which showed evidence of a previous fire. On entering the lobby, a guest was greeted with several old, threadbare Oriental rugs and two worn leather sofas. A porter tagged our luggage, and it was delivered to our respective rooms. A short hallway led from the lobby to the dining room from which the smell of food wafted into the lobby. I could feel my stomach growl.

After completing registration, we returned to the bus that took us the short distance to Gnomewood Links. On the trip, Dick pointed out

Excelsior House, a gray, two-story, stone building with several chimneys and a wide entranceway. Sir Harold and his wife Dorothy reside there when at Gnomewood.

The sun was just appearing through the mist as we departed the bus. The links, a brilliant green color of various shades, stood out along the North Sea. Between the fairways, vegetable patches could be distinguished. The clubhouse was a single-story brick building, painted white, with green trim around two large bay windows facing the links. Between the windows was a doorway that opened onto a large veranda on which there were several white wicker chairs. Those playing in the tournament retrieved their golf bags from the luggage bay beneath the bus. We walked to the clubhouse to register and obtain a small identification tag that would allow for the use of the clubhouse during the tournament. Inside the clubhouse, there was a jovial mood as old friends and competitors greeted one another.

Already on the practice range were several players who had arrived earlier. After Dick had placed his clubs in a locker, we walked to the nearby practice range where we could observe the form of those practicing. Dick pointed out the importance of determining the distance each club would produce. Most players chose driver, 3-wood, 3-iron, 6-iron, 8- or 9-iron, wedge, and putter for their seven clubs. Some sportswriters chose a 5-wood instead of a 3-iron. For the irons, it was important to determine how far a 3-iron went when one eased up on their swing or choked down on the grip. Thus a 3-iron could be used in place of a 4-iron or 5-iron. The same was true for the other irons. This was particularly important for the pros who could win prize money for being on the winning team.

In walking along the range, I could easily identify the professionals by the size of their golf bags and the manufacturer's name on the bag. The pro's name was on the ball pouch. For the sportswriters, the golf bag of choice was a small canvas bag just large enough to hold the seven clubs, golf balls, umbrella, and rain jacket plus towel. For the most part, the pros were hitting the ball long and straight with their drivers. Dick introduced me to the pro, Andy Quickfoot, who was on the winning team last year with the writer Mel Camberwick. Several pros, who were nearby and watching Andy hammer out drives, muttered that he looked like a winner, when he paused to tee up a ball.

Dick said the pairings and tee times for tomorrow would not be posted until this evening or early tomorrow morning. In making up the schedule, Sir Harold tried to avoid known antagonisms between certain sportswriters and pros. Certainly there were instances when a writer might describe a poorly played shot as being "not up to par," but in one instance, a writer described a particular pro as a "paragon of golf ineptitude." That pro refused to talk with that sportswriter for the rest of the golf season. A common criticism aimed at certain pros was "bad nerves." The player didn't need to be reminded of the increased tension associated with a critical putt. Some writers, who had minimal contact with golf professionals during and after a round, tended to write hazy descriptions of what they had witnessed, while other writers, who were familiar with the players, wrote insightful accounts of a particular player and tournament.

As we continued our walk along the practice range, Dick remarked that any of the pros we had observed would make a very acceptable partner for the sportswriter. With that said, he decided it was time for him to start practice, and he returned to the clubhouse to pick up his clubs. I remained on the range, observing pros and sportswriters hitting wedges, irons, and drivers. One pro did stand out from the others. As I learned later, it was Dr. Carrington Middlefield, a former dentist who had been an outstanding golfer on his university team. Later, after finishing dental school, he practiced dentistry for a year but found it dull and lacking the thrill of competition that professional golf would provide. Hence, he turned professional and experienced immediate success. He was tall and made use of his height by having a wide swing arc and accelerating beautifully through the ball. Watching him for a few minutes, I thought any sportswriter paired with him would have a marked advantage in the upcoming tournament.

I noted another golfer near the far end of the practice range who was hitting drives close to 240 yards. Walking closer, I could see it was a young lady. She showed a smooth, seemingly effortless swing that reminded me of motion pictures I had seen of Miss Joyce Wethered, an outstanding British amateur golfer in the 1920s. Watching her hit golf balls, I speculated she was good enough to be considered for Great Britain's Curtis Cup team. After a few minutes, she gave her driver to a young girl holding her golf bag who handed her an iron. She then proceeded to hit balls to the 150-yard marker, all the shots landing within a few yards of the target. When Dick returned with his clubs, I asked him about her. He said her name was Miss Forsythia Shotwell, and Sir Harold had invited her to observe the tournament and possibly be a contestant in the future. He agreed with my assessment of her ability to hit a golf ball. I assumed I would get to meet her later in the clubhouse.

I watched Dick practice for several minutes. He was hitting 6-iron shots and varying the distance by shortening his back swing or shortening his grip, thus producing the result of a 7-iron, then 8-iron. Finally, he took his driver and began hitting shots near the 240-yard mark. Several drives drifted to his left, and he opened his stance slightly to correct this. When he seemed satisfied with the results, he said we should return to the clubhouse for a beer. There we enjoyed our beer and joined a table with two writers who would be playing in the tournament, Lincoln Chatsworth and Fowler Thistltoe. They had competed previously at Gnomewood and felt they had let their pro partners down by poor putting. Both said they had been practicing as often as their work allowed and looked forward to this year's tournament.

Dick motioned another golfer, who had just entered the clubhouse, to join our table. His name was Cyril Popinjay, and Dick asked what *nom de plume* he intended to use. Cyril had previously signed his column as "Bob Cervantes" and had played at Gnomewood under that name. However, Cyril said the popularity of his writing in the *Leister Sports Reporter* had led enough readers to inquire about his real identity. When it was revealed, his popularity only increased. Subsequently, he was invited to compete again in Sir Harold's tournament, although he admitted he hadn't been much help to his partner in previous tournaments, and his handicap was probably higher than fourteen. On hearing this confession, Chatsworth said, "I thought so."

At this point, Miss Shotwell entered the clubhouse, a privilege not usually granted to ladies except on certain weekends. Her sister Rose decided to ride back to Excelsior House with Leffingwell. Everyone stood up to greet her and offer her a place at the table. One young writer, Geoff Cloverjoy, was the first to escort her to the table he was sharing with Bob Paltry and Philip Frogwell-Potts. Geoff offered to get her a beer, but she chose a ginger ale instead. I was sitting near enough to their table so I could see her features in some detail. On the driving range, I could see she was tall, about five feet nine or ten. Sitting nearby, I could see she had auburn hair, blue eyes, and a few freckles that complimented her fair complexion. Several other sportswriters moved over to her table and complimented her on how well she was hitting the ball on the practice range. Dick muttered to me that he had interviewed her after a tournament she had won and said how poised she was as she accepted a small trophy and gave a brief speech thanking the tournament sponsors. Other sports reporters covering that tournament expressed the opinion that she could be the next Joyce Wethered. Miss Shotwell was aware of these compliments and said she hoped she could at least play in the shadow of Miss Wethered.

Just then, Sir Harold entered the clubhouse waving several sheets of paper. These were the pairings and starting times for the tournament starting tomorrow. The players rushed to see them as they were posted on a bulletin board by the entrance. There were a few groans from both writers and professionals, who had walked to the clubhouse from the Foggy Shores. I saw Dick was paired with Dr. Middlefield. Dick turned to me and uttered, "We will either win or it will be a disaster." He then explained that the doctor was a talented golfer but could be erratic at times. In a previous Open, he appeared as though he might contend, but a wild driver and an attack of poor putting left him far behind the leaders on the final day. Dick then looked around the clubhouse for Dr. Middlefield, but he was nowhere in sight. Dick knew the doctor had competed at Gnomewood in the past and, hopefully, would remember on which holes trouble lurked. I noted other pairs of writers and pros were leaving for the practice range to evaluate each other's various abilities, even as sunlight was fading.

I was considering leaving for the Prince Rupert when I heard a loud knock on the clubhouse door. This seemed strange because players had been walking in and out of the clubhouse without knocking. From just outside the doorway, I heard a shout, "It's in the bag, driver, spoon, mashie, niblick, glove, and whiskey." Then in marched the Feverhurst Marching Band, all fifteen members. Inside, they played their signature tune, "It's in the Bag." Then they marched to the bar where they were served whiskey. Quickly downing their signature drink, the band reformed, played "God Save the Queen," and marched out. There was scattered applause from those in the clubhouse. Dick saw the puzzled look on my face and explained the band was a favorite of Sir Harold's and performed at various local events. At times, they had been performing at an earlier event and were somewhat inebriated when they showed up for the golf tournament at Gnomewood. Their sound then was less than tuneful. Dick assured me they would not appear again until next year. It was now getting dark, and I was feeling tired. I saw that Dick wanted to stay and talk with a few writers, and I told him I wanted to return to the hotel.

Back at the Prince Rupert, I intended to take a quick nap before heading down to dinner; however, my quick nap lasted about two hours. I was awakened by the noise generated from returning sportswriters who were enjoying various spirits at the bar, the Brunch of Carrots. I ventured downstairs and decided to avoid the bar and go straight to the dining room. I found a place at a table where three writers were seated, Mel Camberwick, whom I had met earlier, and Philip Frogwell-Potts and Harlow Houndstooth. All had played in Sir Harold's tournament in the past and hoped, as a visiting Yank, I would enjoy watching this year's competition. I asked who would be considered a favorite this year. They all expressed the opinion that it was almost impossible to predict a winning team. The sportswriters were frequently unpredictable in their play. One year, a team had a seven-hole lead starting on the back nine and lost. Poor putting and inept bunker play doomed them. Mel added that last year in the finals, their opponents started to argue over certain shots, and the sportswriter couldn't hit a particular shot under pressure. And some pros simply aren't used to being paired with a less skilled partner in foursomes. After dinner, I excused myself and returned to my room for a shower in a makeshift stall. At least I had a private bath. Before going to bed, I reviewed the program listing the players and the links.

In the morning, the sun was shining through scattered clouds. I glanced out the window to see what pedestrians were wearing. Most wore a jacket or sweater. I decided to wear a windbreaker over a sweater and then headed for the dining room. I saw Dick at a table, and he motioned for me to join him, along with two others. At the table were Bob Paltry, decked out in yellow slacks and yellow sweater, and Charleton Hicks-Joly wearing gray on gray. A waitress brought sliced apples, a large plate of various cheeses, muffins, and a large pot of tea. As we ate, Dick expressed concern about when Dr. Middlefield would appear. Even though their tee time wasn't until eleven thirty, Dick hoped to discuss strategy for playing certain holes. Hicks-Joly speculated the doctor might be practicing at nearby Whinsfield, a nearby nine-hole course. He added he had known the doctor at university, and he was known for showing up for a match shortly before his tee time. Dick agreed he might be practicing at a nearby site.

After breakfast, we enjoyed a smoke before leaving the dining room and stepping outside to board the bus. Arriving at Gnomewood Links, Dick spotted the doctor and his caddie, Bobby Clambourne, at the far end of the practice range. I walked with Dick to where the doctor was practicing, and when the doctor paused to change clubs, Dick introduced me. I saw the doctor was tall, over six feet. He paused from his warm-up and asked me my impression of golf in Great Britain. I replied that in reporting on the Open on two occasions, I thought the golf played was at a high level, but to compete successfully in the States, a golfer faced stiff competition. The doctor realized that and replied that at some point he might travel to the States and compete in our US Open or at least try to qualify. I said I was sure he would qualify. That said, he then resumed practice. I watched him hit drives in the 275–280-yard range, with a smooth, powerful swing. I concluded that, if he and Dick were on their game, they would be favorites to win the Gnomewood Seven-Club Challenge.

CHAPTER 3

Before the tournament started, I briefly reviewed the layout of Gnomewood Links.

Hole 1. Artichoke. The hole is a par-4 of four hundred yards and descends slightly to an elevated green. A bunker guards the green on the right. On the right side of the fairway, a plot of artichokes extends to just short of the bunker. A ball landing in the vegetables is played as ground under repair, and the ball is dropped a club length from the site where the ball entered the vegetables, no nearer the hole. This local rule applied to all vegetable-growing areas.

Hole 2. Asparagus. The hole is a par-4 of 385 yards, with a slight dogleg right. Bunkers guard both sides of the green. Beginning about 150 yards from the tee is a growth of asparagus that extends along the rough.

Hole 3. Beet. The hole is a par-5 dogleg left, measuring 503 yards. A large bunker lies on the left where the fairway begins to bend. A large plot of beets lies along the right side of the fairway. A deep bunker lies behind the green. A drive to where the fairway bends left leaves a fairway wood or long iron to the green and a chance for a birdie.

Hole 4. Broccoli. This is a par-3 of 165 yards. The green slopes back to front and is guarded by bunkers right, left, and behind the green. A patch of broccoli lies outside the left bunker.

Hole 5. Cabbage. The hole is a par-4 of 390 yards. A cabbage patch lies on the right side of the fairway and extends about one hundred yards. On the left side of the fairway are two pot bunkers about 220 yards from the tee. The green is relatively small, with a slight elevation in the middle that tends to repel a poorly hit shot.

Hole 6. Carrot. This hole is a 410-yard par-4 sharp dogleg left. There is a dense growth of elephant grass in the rough where the fairway bends left. On the right side of the fairway is a growth of carrots that extends nearly to the green. A bunker guards the right side of the green. There is a one-stroke penalty for removing a carrot.

Hole 7. Celery. This is a 430-yard par-4 slight dogleg left. There is a growth of celery beginning about 220 yards from the tee that runs along the left side of the fairway. Where the fairway bends left is a long, narrow bunker. The large green is guarded by bunkers right and left.

Hole 8. Cucumber. This hole is a 152-yard par-3 that plays to an elevated green, sloping left to right. A cucumber patch lies along the fairway on the left, and a bunker guards the green on the right.

Hole 9. Eggplant. The hole is a 525-yard par-5 dogleg left. Two shallow bunkers lie where the fairway bends left at the 250-yard mark. Along the fairway in the right rough is a long patch of eggplant. The green is guarded by two pot bunkers on the right. Par is an acceptable score as the hole generally plays into the wind.

Hole 10. Lentil. The hole is a 404-yard par-4 dogleg right. At the crux of the bend on the right is a large hourglass-shaped bunker. On the left side of the fairway is a patch of lentil plants about one hundred yards in length. Because the hole generally plays downwind, some players choose a 3-wood off the tee.

Hole 11. Lettuce. This is a 212-yard par-3, usually playing into the wind. The green is large enough to accept a long iron or 5-wood. A lettuce growth follows beside the fairway on the right. Two bunkers guard the right side of the green. A long iron is the preferred club with which to play this hole.

Hole 12. Parsley. This 365-yard par-4 usually plays downwind, making it a hole where a birdie is a definite possibility. Behind the green is a deep bunker created by a German bomb during the war. Parsley is grown in the rough along both sides of the fairway.

Hole 13. Onion. This is the shortest hole on the links, measuring 145 yards. The green is relatively small and guarded by a bunker on the right and a large gaping bunker behind it, another result of a German bomb. An onion patch lies beside the fairway on the left.

Hole 14. Mustard. This hole is a par-5 of 517 yards. There is a slight dogleg left, and a growth of mustard lies beside the fairway at the dogleg. Two bunkers lie along the right side of the fairway about 240 yards from the tee. The green slopes from back to front and is large enough to accept a fairway wood.

Hole 15. Pea. This is a 185-yard par-3 that plays to a green sloping right to left. A growth of pea plants lies along both sides of the fairway. Two pot bunkers lie on either side of the green, and behind the green is a deep bunker, the former site of an antiaircraft gun.

Hole 16. Potato. This is a four-hundred-yard par-4. A large potato patch lies along the right side of the fairway, in the middle of which is a bunker, also the former site of an antiaircraft gun.

Hole 17. Spinach. This is a par-4 of 440 yards, usually playing into the wind, and is regarded as one of the most difficult to score par. Spinach plants lie along the rough on the right, and a single bunker guards the green on the right.

Hole 18. Tomato. This is a 565-yard par-5 dogleg right. Tomato plants lie on either side of the fairway in the rough. The large green is flanked by bunkers right and left. The hole usually plays downwind, and a long hitter has a chance at a birdie.

Finally, it was my impression that a player has considerable leeway in determining where to drop a ball that landed in the vegetables, particularly if the ball can't be found easily. The vegetables are considered as ground under repair. The player then estimates where the ball crossed into the vegetables and drops it one club length, no closer to the hole. I noted the rough along the vegetables appears to be two or three inches deep, so the next shot from where a ball was dropped won't be easy.

Having reviewed Gnomewood Links, I turned my attention to the contestants warming up on the practice range. The first match is between the team of Geoff Cloverjoy and Byford Barleycroft versus Lincoln Chatsworth and Brace Hardy. Barleycroft has a muscular build and stands well over six feet. His swing is sudden, explosive, and powerful. I noted a tendency to hook. His drives appeared to travel in the 270-to-280-yard range. He is wearing bright red slacks, which should make him easy to spot on the links. Cloverjoy has a smooth, even tempo swing that finishes in balance. He is wearing green slacks and a tan golf shirt.

Lincoln Chatsworth is tall, slender, and primarily an arm swinger, with minimal body movement. Swinging his arms around his body produced a windmill-like appearance. His pro partner, Brace Hardy, has an athletic build and a smooth, compact swing, a style not prone to mistakes. Hardy's caddie is Ken "Knutty" Baldridge, who has had previous experience at Gnomewood and should help the team navigate around the course.

The pros, for the most part, had tan, weather-beaten faces, while the sportswriters tended to appear somewhat pale, indicating time spent indoors hovering over a typewriter. At least, covering a golf tournament offered some exposure to sunlight.

The first group was on the putting green when Sir Harold sounded a horn, indicating they were due on the first tee. On the tee was the announcer, Harley Bellows, a former BBC announcer who possessed a booming, mellifluous voice. He announced Byf Barleycroft as a well-known pro from Eastbourne.

Dick told me the pro usually leads off so that the team gets off to a good start and the sportswriter avoids "first-tee jitters." Barleycroft took several practice swings, and then he blasted a long drive that hooked beyond the rough and landed on a utility road, clearly out of bounds. He started to tee up another ball when Sir Harold reminded him that they were playing alternate shot, and it was now their opponents' play. Brace Hardy then stepped on the tee, took two practice swings, and drove the ball 240 yards down the middle.

Now it was Cloverjoy's turn on the tee. He hadn't counted on his partner driving out of bounds, and he would now be driving off the first tee. He took several tentative practice swings before aiming down the fairway. I noted he was gripping and regripping his driver as he prepared to swing. He took one last look down the fairway, and then he swung and completely missed the ball. He whiffed. Someone in the small gallery yelled, "You're still away!" This brought scattered laughter from the spectators. Both Cloverjoy and Barleycroft were red-faced. Sir Harold then stepped on the tee and reminded Barleycroft it was now his shot. Barleycroft stared angrily at the gallery before teeing up his ball. This time, he blasted a drive of some 270 yards down the left-center of the fairway. Brief applause greeted this effort. Barleycroft bowed to the gallery, and then he and Cloverjoy proceeded down the fairway to play their next shot.

I considered following Cloverjoy and Barleycroft, but I decided it was highly unlikely their performance on the first tee would be repeated on subsequent holes. Instead, I decided to watch the next few teams tee off. Next on the tee was the team of the writer Simon Bumly and pro Devereaux Dedmon versus Derick Marblehead and pro David Duckworth. I watched Bumly on the practice range. He hit the ball with a lunging motion, but it seemed repeatable. Dedmon—with his thin mustache, squinting eyes, and golf cap pulled down over his forehead—resembled what I would imagine Hollywood casting him as a riverboat gambler. He demonstrated a flawless golf swing and pounded the ball 250 yards down the middle.

The next match was between Fowler Thistletoe and the pro Pylton Suggs versus Philip Frogwell-Potts and his pro partner, Giles Nippengay.

Nippengay had been an outstanding amateur and had only recently turned professional. Suggs was on the tee. I had watched him on the practice range, and he demonstrated a short, compact swing. Now he drove the ball some 260 yards into the artichoke patch. Nippengay was next to drive, and he smacked a shot some 240 yards in the fairway. As they left the tee, I noticed Suggs's partner, Thistletoe, wearing plus fours with stockings of green, puce, and umber. A woman standing next to me identified these somewhat unusual colors of his stockings as not found in any rainbow. As Thistletoe searched for his partner's drive, I concluded that any stains from the plants on his stockings would be hard to discern. I wondered if that was the reason he chose this attire.

Dick's match was coming up soon, and I glanced back at the practice range where he was hitting short irons. There was no Dr. Middlefield accompanying him, but because of their later starting time, I suspected the doctor would arrive soon. A few minutes later, I heard the roar of a sports car. Shortly after, I watched as the car parked by the clubhouse and from it emerged the doctor and his caddy Bobby Clambourne. He took the doctor's clubs and walked to the practice range, while the doctor entered the clubhouse, emerging with a drink in his hand. After downing his beverage, he joined his caddy on the range. I felt relieved at the doctor's appearance, and I'm sure Dick did too.

I turned my attention back to the first tee where Cyril Popinjay and Tommy Sapwood were competing against Bob Paltry and Hamilton Smart. Paltry stood out in his yellow attire: yellow visor, yellow golf shirt, and yellow slacks. "You look like a canary," someone shouted. "Lemon drop" was another reference to Bob's appearance. Their opponents both shook their heads negatively after staring at Paltry. This brought a laugh from the gallery. Harley Bellows then stepped to the tee as the laughter subsided and announced the players. Sapwood then took his stance on the tee and, after a practice swing, smacked a drive some 260 yards. Hamilton Smart followed with a drive of 250 yards, and the game was on.

The next group on the tee were two Scotsmen, Ian Crankshaw and Colin Feathershanks, versus Christopher Thinwood and Thatcher Reed. The Scotsmen made a colorful pair. Crankshaw, the sportswriter wore green plus fours with argyle stockings of green, yellow, and dark blue. Feathershanks's plus fours were a checkered pattern of red, yellow, and blue, with dark blue stockings. Both wore dark blue tams. Feathershanks had the honors. He stroked a drive of 250 yards down the middle. Reed followed with a drive of some 260 yards.

There were several more groups to tee off, but rather than watch them drive, I decided to walk to the sixth hole and watch the sportswriters hit their drives. I was interested in how the two teams would play this dogleg hole with elephant grass on the left and the growth of carrots on the right. Approaching the sixth tee, I could see the red slacks of Byf Barleycroft finishing putting on the fifth hole. This group then moved on to the tee where Lincoln Chatsworth teed up his ball. His pro partner, Brace Hardy, pointed down the right side of the fairway, the safer side. Chatsworth took two tentative practice swings and then drove the ball into the carrots. Cloverjoy was next to hit. Barleycroft also pointed to the right side of the fairway, away from the danger on the left. Cloverjoy nervously gripped and regripped his driver, took a final look down the fairway, and hooked his drive into the elephant grass. Barleycroft could be seen muttering to Cloverjoy as the players left the teeing area.

After several minutes searching for Cloverjoy's drive, Barleycroft found the ball in the high grass. He quickly decided the ball was unplayable and took back-of-the-line relief. He then played their third shot to the green with a midiron. Now it was Hardy's shot. After retrieving Chatsworth's drive from the carrots, he dropped it a club length from the edge of the carrot patch and lofted an 8-iron to the green. On the green, Cloverjoy had a par putt of about fifteen feet from the flag. He and Barleycroft lined it up, and then Cloverjoy stroked it about two feet short. Chatsworth now had two putts for par and to win the hole. His putt just missed on the right and tricked a foot beyond. This short putt was conceded, and Chatsworth and Hardy were 2-up.

Next to appear on the sixth tee was Si Bumly. I was told by a spectator that Bumly and Dedmon were 1-up. Bumly waved his driver back and forth several times before teeing up his ball. Dedmon pointed down the right side of the fairway and then patted his partner on the back. Bumly then addressed the ball and lunged forward, removing a generous amount of turf and advancing the ball about 180 yards down the fairway. This left his partner with a long iron shot to the green.

Next to hit was the sportswriter Derick Marblehead. He was a free-swinger, and after several vigorous practice swings, he slammed a drive into the elephant grass. Marblehead conferred with his pro partner, Duckworth, and they decided to declare a lost ball and take a one-stroke penalty and loss of distance. Duckworth then teed up a new ball and blasted a drive of some 260 yards down the middle. The next shot was Dedmon's. He struck a 3-iron to just short of the green, leaving Bumly with a straight chip shot to the flagstick.

Marblehead was next to play. He made amends for his poor drive by lofting a midiron to about eight feet from the flag. Bumly was next to play, and he chipped to within two feet of the cup. Duckworth now lined up their par-saving eight-footer. After several practice strokes, he putted and missed on the left side of the cup. Their remaining putt was conceded. Dedmon stood over the winning par putt before it was conceded. He and Bumly were now 2-up.

Now on the sixth tee was the golf writer Philip Frogwell Potts. As with the previous teams, the pro partner, Giles Nippengay, pointed away from the high grass on the left. I had noted in practice that Frogwell-Potts tended to hook his drives, which was not the shot a golfer wanted on this hole. As I suspected, F-P hit a drive that hugged the right side of the fairway before hooking left into the elephant grass. Their opponents, Fowler Thistletoe and Pylton Suggs, watched the drive disappear into the grass, and then Thistletoe stepped to the tee. He took two practice swings and stroked a gentle fade into the carrots. The two teams approached their respective drives, and Suggs quickly found the ball in the carrots. He appeared to be away, so he struck a 6-iron to about ten feet from the flag.

Meanwhile, F-P and Nippengay were searching in the elephant grass for F-P's drive. The ball was found after several minutes, and Nippengay decided to declare an unplayable lie. He dropped the ball a club length from the high grass, in the rough, and lofted a midiron to about twelve feet from the flag. On the green, F-P was slightly away. His par putt just missed on the right. Thistletoe lined up his birdie putt and stroked it to the edge of the cup, leaving a par tap-in. Thistletoe and Suggs were now 1-up.

The next two groups halved the hole, Ian Crankshaw and Colin Feathershanks retaining their 1-up lead, and last year's winning team of Mel Camberwick and Andy Quickfoot retaining their 1-up lead.

I decided to wait by the sixth green for Dick's group. Looking back at the tee, I saw the purple slacks and lavender sweater of Livingston Phogg-Smythe. His colorful attire didn't enhance his golf game. He had a loop, even a double loop, in his backswing that resulted in a flailing motion as he swung. His drive sliced over the carrots into deep rough farther to the right. Next to hit was Harlow Houndstooth. His swing was short and quick, and he drove the ball straight down the fairway. In the rough, Phogg-Smythe and his partner, Cliff Halestork, found the drive and proceeded to trade attempts to blast the ball from the rough before Halestork picked up the ball, conceding the hole.

Finally, I saw Dick on the sixth tee. Dick appeared loose and relaxed, indicating to me that he and the doctor were playing well. He took his stance on the tee and then swung. His drive landed on the fairway where the dogleg bends left about 240 yards from the tee. Maynard Cumbersome was next. Perhaps trying to match Dick's drive, he attempted to play a draw around the dogleg but hooked the ball into the elephant grass. Watching the players all morning, I had seen several instances of a drive not clearing the grass, and this led to that team's losing the hole.

Cumbersome's partner, Fossilgrass, quickly declared a lost ball and teed up another. He drove this ball 250 yards down the middle. The players marched down the fairway to where Dick's drive had landed. The doctor then stroked a midiron to the green. Cumbersome was now up, and he hit a wobbly iron that landed several yards short of the green. His pro partner, Hew Fossilgrass, then chipped to about five feet from the cup. Dick now had a ten-foot putt for a birdie. He lined it up and stroked it, just missing on the right. Cumbersome now had a five-foot putt for bogie. He looked at the line, stepped up, and missed the cup by several inches. Dick and the doctor were now 2-up.

As we walked off the sixth green, I asked Dick and the doctor if a player could declare a lost ball without looking for it. The doctor said a provisional ball could be hit, but it was likely the drive in the elephant grass was lost or unplayable, and to avoid wasting time, Fossilgrass hit another drive. In a sense, this could be the provisional ball.

The seventh hole was halved with par—as was the short eighth hole. The ninth hole, a 525-yard par-5, presented a challenge. The breeze was into the player's face, and two deep bunkers guard the left side of the fairway where it bends slightly to the left. A growth of eggplant parallels the fairway on the right for about 150 yards.

Dr. Middlefield was now on the tee. After a quick practice stroke, he slammed a drive some 260 yards down the left-center of the fairway. Fossilgrass followed and smacked a drive of about 250 yards that drifted into the eggplant. He and Cumbersome found the drive. Cumbersome lifted the ball out and dropped it in the rough a club length from his reference point. He took one fierce practice swing with his 3-wood and drilled a shot that dropped into a pot bunker short of the green.

The next shot was Dick's. He selected his 3-wood and hit a shot that appeared headed for the green but caught the wind and dropped about fifty feet short. After determining who was away, the doctor was next to play. He lofted a wedge shot that landed and rolled to about six feet from the flag. Fossilgrass now had a shot from the bunker. He was close enough to the edge so that he had to open the blade on his wedge to gain enough elevation to escape from the bunker. He blasted a high shot that landed on the edge of the green and stopped about thirty feet from the flagstick. The two sportswriters had birdie putts, but Dick's was much shorter. Cumbersome and Fossilgrass surveyed their putt. Fossilgrass then pointed about two inches outside the left edge as an aiming point. Cumbersome stroked a putt that appeared on a line but broke off to the right just before the cup. The remaining putt was conceded. Dick had the six-footer for a birdie. He and the doctor conferred briefly before Dick took his stance and then stroked a putt that I thought for certain would drop, but it stopped on the edge. After about a minute, the doctor was ready to tap in the putt, but Fossilgrass conceded the putt. Thus, neither team was able to score a birdie on this par-5 hole.

A refreshment cart had been placed between the ninth green and tenth tee. The two sportswriters selected cheese plates and lemonade, the doctor grabbed two beers, and Fossilgrass chose a sausage sandwich and a beer. After about ten minutes, the snacks were consumed, and Dick stepped to the tee. The tenth hole measured 404 yards in length, with a dogleg right. A large bunker lay where the fairway bent right. Lentils grew along the left side of the fairway. The hole was playing downwind, and the doctor suggested that Dick hit his 3-wood off the tee to avoid the large bunker. Dick agreed and stroked a drive that landed just short of the bunker.

Cumbersome was now on the tee. He decided to use his driver, and after a practice swing, he slammed a drive some 250 yards down the middle, his best drive of the match so far. Dick's drive left the doctor with a shot of some 175 yards. He played a midiron that caught the wind, landed at the back of the green, and then tricked off into a bunker behind the green.

Next to hit was Fossilgrass. He struck a 7-iron to about fifteen feet from the flag. I didn't know how good a bunker player Dick was, but I hoped he would blast out, leaving a relatively short putt for par. Dick's explosion shot nearly hit the flagstick but rolled some fifteen feet beyond. I had an uneasy feeling Dick and the doctor might lose the hole. Cumbersome has an uphill putt of about fifteen feet for birdie. The next putt was the doctor's. He stroked a good putt, but it missed on the left. The remaining putt was conceded. Cumbersome now had a chance to hit the winning putt. He lined it up and nearly sank it, leaving a short putt for par and a win. Dick and the doctor were now just 1-up. The doctor left the green muttering they shouldn't have lost a relatively easy hole.

The eleventh hole, a par-3 of 212 yards, was halved with bogies. Both pros missed the green with 3-irons, and neither Cumbersome nor Dick hit chip shots anywhere near the cup. Both pros missed par putts.

The twelfth hole is 365 yards and plays downwind, making it a possible birdie hole. Parsley lines both sides of the fairway, and a large bunker guards the green on the right. Cumbersome teed off first. He let fly a long drive that landed in the parsley. Dick, now on the tee, hit a 3-wood that landed in the fairway. Fossilgrass found his partner's drive. He looked around to find an advantageous spot to drop the ball but found none; therefore, he dropped it in rough some three inches high. Using a lofted club, he blasted out, landing in a deep bunker right of the green.

The doctor was next to hit. He lofted a wedge to about five feet from the flag. Meanwhile, Cumbersome had climbed down into the bunker, and after several practice swings, he blasted a shot that barely cleared the lip of the bunker, leaving a putt of some thirty feet for par. Fossilgrass now had to make this putt for par. He lined it up and stroked a putt that missed on the left. Dick now had a five-foot putt for birdie. His putt stopped on the lip, leaving a tap-in for par and a win. He and the doctor were now 2-up.

The short thirteenth hole was halved with par. The fourteenth hole was a 517-yard par-5 playing into the wind. A growth of mustard lines the right side of the fairway, and three bunkers lie along the left. Dick stood on the tee judging where to aim his tee shot. The doctor pointed right-center, thus avoiding the first bunker on the left. Dick then hit a controlled fade that landed on the edge of the right rough.

Cumbersome was now up. He took several practice swings and then blooped a drive that landed in the mustard. Cumbersome and his partner took several minutes before finding the ball. After retrieving the ball from the mustard, Fossilgrass dropped the ball in the rough and hammered a 3-wood some 240 yards down the fairway. The doctor selected a 3-wood from his caddie and struck a long shot that landed just short of the green. Cumbersome was next to play. He struck a short iron that landed some twenty feet from the flagstick. Now it was Dick's turn. He selected an 8-iron and played a low running shot that stopped about three feet from the hole. Fossilgrass now had a twenty-foot putt for birdie. His putt just missed on the right. Now it was up to the doctor to sink the birdie putt. He took a drag on his cigarette before lining up the putt, took his stance, and stroked the putt in the cup for a birdie and a 3-up lead.

As I left the area around the fourteenth green, I saw a stone marker on which the following inscription was carved: "On this site on 3 March 1945, Major Harold Gilroy captured singlehandedly a German submarine.

This heroic action saved countless Allied ships from destruction." I would learn later about this heroic action.

The short par-3 fifteenth hole was halved with par. The match was now dormie. The sixteenth hole is a par-4 of four hundred yards, playing downwind. A potato patch lay to the right of the fairway, in the middle of which was a deep bunker caused by a German bomb. Both Dick and Cumbersome hit 3-woods off the tee to avoid hitting into the bunker. Dick's drive was about ten yards shorter, leaving the doctor with a short-iron to the green. He struck a wedge to the lower edge of the green, thus avoiding going long and possibly causing the ball to trickle off the green into a deep bunker.

Fossilgrass now had a wedge shot to the green, and he hammered a high shot that landed beyond the flag and rolled to the edge of the green. I thought this left Cumbersome with a nearly impossible putt to try to roll near the flagstick since the green sloped from back to front. The doctor walked to the back of the green to inspect their opponent's putt and then returned to where Dick was sizing up his putt of about twenty feet. I could see Cumbersome's putter swinging back and forth as he practiced his long downhill putt. He then stroked the putt. Fossilgrass watched his partner's putt that rolled some fifteen feet below the flag. Dick had been lining up his putt, and, after the putt by Cumbersome, he took two practice strokes and rolled a putt about a foot from the cup. This remaining putt by Fossilgrass was long by two feet, and the match was conceded with Dick and the doctor winning three and two.

After congratulatory handshakes, I heard Dick tell Cumbersome that he couldn't have putted much closer either. The four walked to the clubhouse for refreshments. In the clubhouse, there was a buzz about what had happened that caused a brief delay in the match preceding Dick's. Phogg-Smythe and Halestork won that match. I saw Halestork, Houndstooth, and Taylor having a beer, but no Phogg-Smythe. My inquiry about the missing member of their foursome was answered by only smiles. Halestork then related what had caused the delay. Phogg-Smythe was in the deep rough on sixteen. He took several vigorous practice swings and then blasted out, the ball landing on the green, along with bits of grass and turf. On the green, Phogg-Smythe mumbled something about his teeth. Apparently, his dentures flew out of his mouth when he swung. Halestork said he saw his partner pick up something among the pieces of turf and put it in his pocket. Just then Phogg-Smythe emerged from the men's room, teeth in place. He explained he had finished washing his dentures to remove bits of dirt. He saw the doctor at our table and asked the doctor if he had retained some of his training from dental school and could he recommend some dental adhesive. Dr. Middlefield immediately recommended Dr. Molar's Dental Fixative. Grafton overheard the conversation and volunteered to drive to Gnomewood and obtain this dental product from a well-stocked apothecary. He returned shortly, and Phogg-Smythe was able to insert his dentures and smile confidently.

"It was a toothless victory," someone yelled.

Further conversation in the clubhouse revealed that Bob Paltry had temporarily lost his visor and toupee in a gust of wind. He quickly recovered his visor, but the hairpiece had landed in the rough where a stray dog found it and ran around looking for the hunter who had downed it. After much coaxing with a sausage, the dog finally dropped the hairpiece and gobbled down the sausage. Paltry then grabbed his "rug" and stuffed it in his golf bag. The match then proceeded, but Paltry's game was off, and he and his partner, Hamilton Smart, lost to Cyril Popinjay and Tommy Sapwood four and three.

The other competitors were gathering around the scoreboard, sizing up their opponents for tomorrow's matches. Dick and the doctor would be competing against Phogg-Smythe and Halestork. The two Scotsmen, Ian Crankshaw and Colin Feathershanks, were facing Mel Camberwick and Andy Quickfoot, last year's winning team. Philip Frogwell-Potts and Giles Nippengay were competing against Cyril Popinjay and Tommy Sapwood, and, in the last match, Geoff Cloverjoy and Byford Barleycroft were facing Si Bumly and Deveraux Dedmon.

After everyone had reviewed tomorrow's matches, several players suggested we return to the hotel. A voice exclaimed, "Paltry needs to shampoo his rug." There were a few chuckles as we started out the door. We passed the putting green where Cloverjoy and Miss Shotwell were engaged in a putting contest. Back at the hotel, I asked Geoff who was the winner. He replied somewhat sheepishly that Miss Shotwell was the winner.

CHAPTER 4

Back at the hotel, Christopher Thinwood commented that even if he and his partner, Thatcher Reed, had won their match, he felt so fatigued he didn't think he could play tomorrow. Dick reminded him that tournament golf could be tiring, and that is one reason Sir Harold conceived this tournament so writers could feel how enervating golf competition could be. Several others chimed in, voicing how tired they were and looking forward to dinner and a good night's sleep.

Once inside the hotel, we all decided to combat fatigue by visiting the Bunch of Carrots. Leffingwell and Sir Harold joined us, having ridden to the hotel on the motorcycle. They were interested in hearing any complaints about the course or the tournament. There were several complaints about the sixth hole, the elephant grass on the left, and the height of the rough on the right along the carrots. Fowler Thistletoe proposed a drop zone by the carrots. Sir Harold opposed this idea but said he would have Grafton trim the rough around the carrots to about two inches.

Sir Harold also said, "If a drive was seen headed for the elephant grass, the player should hit a provisional ball. This saves time if the search is futile, and the player must return to the tee." Another complaint centered around the deep bunkers, behind the thirteenth and sixteenth greens.

Sir Harold replied, "Those bunkers are the fault of the Germans, and the deep bunkers make the holes more challenging."

While Sir Harold continued discussing various other holes, I noted Leffingwell resting in a corner with a beer and thought this might be an opportunity to question him about the plaque along the shoreline near the fourteenth green. When I brought up the topic, he smiled and said it was an interesting story. He had been discharged from the navy in December 1944 and had rejoined Sir Harold at Gnomewood Links.

On a foggy day in early March 1945, he and Sir Harold were inspecting the links to evaluate damage from the war. There were reports that the Germans had bombed the links on at least one occasion. He and Sir Harold were riding in the motorcycle and sidecar, and as they progressed along the shoreline, a large dark image appeared to have emerged from the water and plowed onto the beach.

Leffingwell immediately identified it as a submarine, and looking closely, they saw a swastika on the conning tower. A figure emerged from the conning tower and then disappeared. They could hear the sub's engine roaring as it attempted to back off the beach.

Sir Harold exclaimed they should return to Excelsior House—where the phone had recently been restored—and notify Coastal Defense. "Then we'll take some weapons and capture the Germans—or at least thwart their invasion attempt."

Leffingwell said, "I don't think this is a good idea because we didn't know what weapons the Germans have on board."

Sir Harold ignored his caution, went to his gun cabinet, unlocked it, and took out his Carrington & Black .505 rhino gun and a Webster .454 Trenchmaster revolver. He stuck the revolver in his waistband and grabbed some ammunition.

They went back to the beach on the motorcycle.

Leffingwell said, "As we approached the beach, we could see several Germans had emerged from the sub and were inspecting their predicament. One of them pointed a pistol at us as we came to a stop about a hundred feet from the hull. Sir Harold jumped from the sidecar and pointed the rhino gun at the Germans. He seemed to recognize one of the Germans wearing an officer's hat and shouted, 'Is that you,

Heinrich?' Sir Harold waded into the surf and pointed the rifle at the Germans. They were still pointing their pistol at us.

"After several seconds, the German in the officer's hat responded, 'Harold?'

"Sir Harold kept wading toward the Germans. He reminded the German officer that they had competed against each other in swimming in the 1936 Olympic games, held in Berlin. Sir Harold shouldered the rhino gun, and the two former competitors met and shook hands. The German sailor holding the pistol lowered it.

"Captain Heinrich eyed the rhino gun, fearing that, if it discharged, the bullet might pierce the hull, or produce a shock wave by the bullet striking the hull that might detonate the forward torpedoes. He muttered something in German to the sailor with the pistol who returned it to his side. Sir Harold lowered his rhino gun and, looking at the sub embedded on the beach, said somewhat factiously, 'A bad bit of seamanship, Heinrich.'

"The captain answered in halting English that he had been chased by a British destroyer and had become confused in the heavy mist. About then, a searchlight from the destroyer appeared in the distance. The captain barked a command to leave the sub—but not before two crew members threw into the surf what were probably logbooks and code instructions. The crew then assembled by the fourteenth green. Sir Harold saw the searchlight from the destroyer approaching and was afraid the destroyer might spot the sub and start shooting, and he motioned for the crew to march inland to the clubhouse.

"In the clubhouse, Sir Harold found several bottles of wine remaining that hadn't been removed at the start of the war. He then opened them and said to the captain, 'We will celebrate your escape.' I thought the word *capture* might be more appropriate, but I didn't say anything.

"Soon, an armored vehicle arrived with soldiers from Coastal

Defense to process the prisoners. The officer in charge was surprised to see the sailors and their officer drinking wine. A prison bus arrived to transport the Germans to a camp farther inland. Before the bus departed, Sir Harold and Heinrich shook hands and vowed to meet after the war."

Somehow, this story became known in Gnomewood, and someone proposed that a plaque be placed where Sir Harold's "heroic action" had saved the village. Sir Harold did not dispute their admiration. The submarine was pulled off the shoreline several days later by a navy tugboat, but not before a boarding party had inspected the interior of the sub to make sure it hadn't been booby-trapped.

I asked Leffingwell about the V-1 flying bomb embedded in the beach near the fourteenth green. He thought it had landed in the fall of 1944. Because it wasn't near a densely populated area, it wasn't immediately disarmed and removed. There it remains to this day. The Royal Engineers' bomb removal squad has examined it several times in recent years and always viewed it at high tide. They concluded the removal of the V-1 was a job for the navy. The navy has approached it at low tide and concluded its removal was a job for the Royal Engineers. So, it rests on the beach and has been a source of interest to passing sailboats. Someone painted "Arsenal Rules" on it several years ago. Whoever did that must have concluded it was safe after twelve plus years on the beach.

The aroma from the kitchen drifted into the Bunch of Carrots, and someone suggested we move to the dining room. Leffingwell excused himself and said he would see me tomorrow. The wood-paneled dining room had been darkened by years of tobacco smoke. Two large ceiling fans wafted away smoke from pipes, cigarettes, and cigars. Light came from ornate wall fixtures that appeared to have dated back to the turn of the century. Several beer and cigarette advertisements on the walls added color to the room.

The featured item on the menu was a Bedfordshire Clanger. I had no idea what that was, but it proved to be a combination of ground pork, apples, mushrooms, and onions. Dick and I sat down at a round table with Maynard Cumbersome and Cyril Popinjay. We commenced discussing the day's play.

Popinjay said the green on the 212-yard eleventh hole wasn't holding a tee shot. His partner Tommy Sapwood hit a 5-wood that landed on the green and bounced off. Sapwood claimed he had hit a 5-wood or 3-iron in past tournaments and held the green. Dick wondered if the hole had been shortened slightly because of its proximity to the coast, and he reminded Popinjay there hadn't been any rain at Gnomewood for over a week—and the green was quite firm.

Cumbersome added that the hole, in his opinion, was best played with a long iron, allowing the ball to bounce onto the green. Popinjay thought this was a sensible suggestion, but he said he thought the pros would still prefer to hit the green with their tee shot. The pros were playing for money, and hitting the green offered the best chance for a birdie.

The subject of the sixth hole came up. Cumbersome thought aiming for the carrots was the best play—even though some damage to the carrots would occur. This was safer than playing to the dogleg and running the risk of having your ball land in the elephant grass. We hoped Sir Harold would tolerate minor damage to the carrots. Cumbersome said he would continue aiming at the carrots, offering his pro partner a safe shot to the green. We decided to bring these issues to Sir Harold's attention tomorrow.

I could hear the pop of champagne corks, and the waitress brought a bottle and glasses to our table. This was followed by the Clanger, which we proceeded to divide up and enjoy. Three glasses of champagne later, I started to feel the need for sleep. All the walking during the tournament produced a pleasant sense of fatigue. I excused myself from the writers and walked through the lobby, noting a weather report that had been posted. It warned of high winds and rain later tonight, tapering by morning. Back in my room, I pulled my rain gear from my suitcase. I assumed I would probably need it in the morning. After a quick shower, I jotted down a few notes about the day's play and was ready for bed.

Shortly after two, I was awakened by a howling wind and rain pelting on the window. I was about to fall asleep again when a tremendous explosion shook the hotel. I arose with some trepidation and went to the window to see if there was any nearby damage. The rain had nearly stopped. From covering police and fire reports as a young reporter, I suspected there may have been a gas explosion in a nearby building. I decided to walk down to the lobby and see if the night clerk had any information as to the cause of the explosion.

In the hallway, I met Ian Crankshaw, in his tartan pajamas, and asked what he thought was the cause of the explosion. He suspected a naval mine from the recent war may have broken loose from its mooring and detonated when it struck the shore. It might have been one of ours or belonged to the Germans.

In the lobby, we were joined by Si Bumly and Mel Camberwick. Mel went to the front door and looked up and down the street. He said he could see no obvious damage. I then recalled that the intensity of the explosion reminded me of the blasts caused by V-1 flying bombs, several of which had landed near the base where I was assigned. Bumly agreed that the intensity of the explosion was no naval mine. He had been stationed at Great Yarmouth during the war, and mines would occasionally wash ashore and explode. This explosion was nothing like that caused by a naval mine.

After a few minutes, Ian suggested a whiskey would be appropriate to help us get back to sleep. The Carrot was closed, but the night clerk agreed to open it. Whiskey or brandy were the choices. I chose whiskey.

The night clerk said he would put on a raincoat and walk to the police station to find out what they knew about the explosion.

After about fifteen minutes, the clerk returned and said the buildings in Gnomewood appeared intact, but one constable was certain the blast had come from the links. With that bit of information, we all felt certain the V-1 had blown up. We finished our drinks and decided there was nothing more we could learn tonight. We thought it best to return to our rooms and get some sleep.

At breakfast, the dining room was abuzz about the explosion. Several suspected the V-1 had blown up, caused by the waves from the storm hitting the shore. Dick wondered if the links would be playable. We quickly ate breakfast and headed for the street entrance of the hotel to see if the bus was there. It was.

CHAPTER 5

At the clubhouse, several of the pros were about to venture onto the links. They told us that Sir Harold, Leffingwell, and Grafton were already on the course, surveying the damage. One of the pros, Andy Quickfoot, said he was sure the explosion was caused by a V-1, or "doodlebug," as the flying bombs were called in England. He had been within a mile from where one exploded, causing considerable damage to a factory,

Dick recommended we walk down the eighteenth fairway to the shoreline and then continue along the beach to where the V-1 had been embedded. We started walking, and as we approached the fourteenth green, we saw Sir Harold, Leffingwell, and Grafton standing between the fourteenth and fifteenth greens This was about where the V-1 had been. A segment of the shoreline was missing, and the edge of the water was now close enough to the fourteenth green so that, in a high wind, waves might wash over the green. Also, shots to the green, if hit too firmly, might end up in the water.

Sir Harold saw us, and before we could start asking questions about the links, he said the course was playable for today's matches. He pointed to a piece of the V-1 that was sticking out of the water close to where the bomb must have exploded. He speculated that this part from the V-1 must have been thrown up in the air in the explosion and come down and stuck below the water level. Sir Harold then said he and his men would continue their inspection of the links, and those playing today should start to warm up.

Two caddies, Knutty Baldridge and Alphie Judson, had been exploring the links on their own, checking for damage. Suddenly, they called out that in the onion patch along the thirteenth fairway, there was a badly burned body, missing a head, an arm, and part of a leg.

Sir Harold and Leffingwell were unaware of this until they heard the caddies' shocking finding. They walked to the onion patch, glanced briefly at the body, rushed to where the motorcycle had been parked, and announced they would go back to Excelsior House and report these findings to law enforcement officials. Several golfers on the practice range saw players and caddies on the course and walked to where we were viewing the body. They joined us in our speculation that the body was the result of the explosion. Dick wondered if this was someone who had crept onto the links to paint another message on the V-1 or perhaps a passing fisherman who the storm had blown too close to shore.

Sir Harold returned and announced the tournament would start in about an hour. "And don't touch the body."

The sportswriters and pros walked quickly back to the clubhouse to obtain their clubs and prepare for day two of the tournament. Practice then began.

The Gnomewood police arrived, followed by law enforcement officers from neighboring Lydston Heath, and Grafton escorted them to the body. A police van arrived and gathered up the remains of the body. Several of the policemen waded out in the surf to inspect the remaining part of the V-1. They quickly concluded the part was from the engine. It had apparently been blown off when the explosive part of the V-1 had detonated. Other policemen continued looking for parts of the body that might help identify it and for other clues as to why the explosion had occurred.

Rather than continue to observe the police, I walked back to the practice range where the golfers were warming up. I assumed I would find out more about the explosion and the body later. On the range, I saw the familiar red slacks of Byf Barleycorn. He and his partner, Cloverjoy, were warming up for their upcoming match against Si Bumly and Devereaux Dedmon. I wondered if Bumly's lunging swing would throw off Barleycroft's game. Among those observing the warmup was Miss Shotwell. Was it a particular interest in Cloverjoy?

Sir Harold sounded a horn and announced the matches were ready to start. Barleycroft strode to the first tee. After a brief introduction, he teed up his ball, and after a ferocious practice swing, he slammed a drive some 270 yards down the middle. No need for Cloverjoy to follow his partner on the tee, as he did yesterday.

Dedmon was next to hit. He stroked a drive of about 250 yards, and the match began. I decided to follow this group and see how the sportswriters played their second shots. The next shot was Bumly's. He selected a midiron and waggled the club a few times before aiming it at the green and lunging at the ball. He connected and sent the ball skyward along with a sizable divot. The shot landed about twenty yards short of the green.

Cloverjoy was next to play. After a practice swing, he lofted an iron shot that landed about fifteen feet from the pin. The next shot was Dedmon's. He played a chip shot from off the green to about three feet from the cup. Barleycroft was now away. Putter in hand, he gazed at the cup for a few seconds before taking his stance and stroking a good putt that just missed. The short remaining putt was conceded. Bumly now had a three-footer to halve the hole. He and Dedmon lined up the putt, and Bumbrey stroked a putt that rolled in dead center. So, they halved the first hole.

I decided to remain by the first green, watch the teams play through, and then continue with Dick and Dr. Middlefield. Glancing at the parking lot, I saw the doctor's Jaguar. He *had* arrived. On the fairway, having just teed off, Cyril Popinjay and Tommy Sapwood were playing against Phil Frogwell-Potts and Giles Nippengay. Frogwell-Potts was first to play. His swing has been described as "attractive indolence." However, today, his swing was more indolent than firm. His shot landed well short of the green, leaving Nippengay with a long chip shot to the flagstick. They would end up losing the hole.

The next match coming down the fairway was that of the two Scotsmen, Ian Crankshaw and Colin Feathershanks, playing against the defending champions, Mel Camberwick and Andy Quickfoot. Crankshaw was away. He lofted a midiron to the back of the green. Quickfoot's drive landed in the rough, leaving Camberwick with a difficult shot. He took several practice swings, swung mightily, and sent the ball and turf about twenty yards short of the green. Feathershanks then played an excellent pitch shot to about five feet from the flag. The hole was ultimately halved as Crankshaw sank the par putt to match their opponent's par.

Now on the fairway was Livingston Phogg-Smythe. His bright lavender sweater was easy to spot. Standing off to the side were Dick and the doctor. With his serpentine backswing, Phogg-Smythe launched a slice that landed in a bunker to the right of the green. Dick then moved forward to play the doctor's drive. He struck a short-iron to about ten feet from the flag. Phogg-Smythe's pro partner, Cliff Halestork, played the bunker shot to about six feet from the cup. The doctor lined up the ten-foot putt, flicked away his cigarette, and sank the putt for a birdie. Dick and the doctor were now 1-up.

I watched the teams tee off on the 385-yard second hole. Both Dick and Phogg-Smythe hit the fairway with their drives. The pros hit the green with their second shots, leaving the writers with birdie putts. Neither sank their putts, and the remaining short putts were conceded.

The third hole was a 503-yard par-5. As we were walking to the tee, we heard a scream from around the area of the seventh green. Dick motioned to me and asked me to hustle over to where the scream seemed to originate and see what had prompted the outburst. I sprinted toward the sound of the scream with a sense of foreboding. Could it have come from Miss Shotwell?

On reaching the seventh green, I saw the red slacks of Barleycroft rushing to the bunker by the green. Lying on the ground beside the bunker was Miss Shotwell. Cloverjoy joined his partner by Miss Shotwell's unconscious body. Cloverjoy quickly removed his golf glove and using it as a fan, began whipping the glove back and forth over her face. Unfortunately, his arc descended slightly causing her face to be slapped several times before she began to regain consciousness and blurt out, "Stop!"

Barleycroft had been standing behind Cloverjoy and pushed his partner away. "Give her air," he shouted, motioning the spectators to move back. He then helped her sit up.

I walked carefully around the bunker, and glancing in it, I saw a burned arm. This must have been the source of her shock. The scorer for the match used his flashlight to signal the clubhouse that help was needed. The first to see it was Soufflé, who interpreted the signal that refreshments were needed. By the time he arrived by the seventh green with a vat of tea, biscuits, and slices of cheese, Miss Shotwell was sitting up and gladly accepted the tea. Being appraised of the situation, Soufflé offered to drive her back to the clubhouse, but she declined, saying she felt well enough to continue following the golf match.

Cloverjoy started to approach her, I suspect to apologize for slapping her with his golf glove, but Barleycroft grabbed his arm and said they should get on with their golf game. It was now his shot. Barleycroft promptly shanked his pitch shot into the bunker near where the arm lay. Now it was Cloverjoy's turn. He stepped into the bunker, eyed the burned arm, and then carefully lined up his shot. He hit a weak explosion that barely cleared the edge of the bunker, leaving Barleycroft with a thirty-foot putt for bogie. Meanwhile, Bumbrey and Dedmon had watched Miss Shotwell's fainting spell and subsequent recovery. Bumbry's second shot had hopped, skipped, and jumped to where Dedmon had a birdie putt of about ten feet. Barleycroft then missed his bogie putt and conceded the hole. Bumbry and Dedmon were now 2-up.

A siren in the distance indicated law enforcement officers were on their way and would soon be arriving. Riding along the front nine on his motorcycle, Sir Harold and Leffingwell were encouraging the players to speed up. Sir Harold paused at the ninth tee and announced he wanted to clear the front nine so a thorough search for body parts and other clues could be made by the law officers. He answered a few questions from golfers who were not aware of why play had been temporarily halted. He added that several members from Scotland Yard and British Military Intelligence would soon be arriving.

Meanwhile, Dedmon and Barleycroft teed off on the ninth hole, a 525-yard par-5. Both drives were in the fairway. The sportswriters managed to hit the second shots down the fairway, leaving the pros with easy wedge shots to the green. The hole was halved with par. Next came the doctor and Halestork on the tee. The doctor hit first and blasted a drive of some 275–280 yards left-center on the fairway. Halestork's drive traveled some 240 yards down the middle. This left Phogg-Smythe with a 3-wood to the green. His shot traveled only about two hundred yards.

Dick was now up. I knew he could hit a 3-wood some 220 yards, which he did. Halestork then hit a wedge that the breeze pushed into one of the pot bunkers guarding the green on the right. The doctor had the next shot. He played a low, running 8-iron that stopped about five feet from the flag. I thought this was the right shot; it stayed below the inconsistent breeze.

Phogg-Smythe had the next shot. He entered the bunker, and after getting advice from his partner, he blasted out some twenty feet beyond the cup. This left Halestork with the twenty-footer for par that he left short. Dick now had the five-footer for birdie. The doctor pointed out where the putt would break slightly to the right. Dick then lined up the putt and sank it for a birdie. He and the doctor were now 3-up.

A small refreshment table had been set up by the tenth tee. We circled the table before Dick took a cup of tea and several cookies. The doctor grabbed a beer that he downed quickly before taking a second. Halestork and Phogg-Smythe took lemon sodas and sausage sandwiches. As a guest, I selected a sausage sandwich and a beer. We ate quickly and silently. The young lady attending the food cart began to place the food and beverages on a tray inside the cart. I asked her if she was going to pull the cart all the way back to the clubhouse, and she replied, "Soufflé will pull the cart back to the clubhouse with the jeep." We finished the refreshments and walked to the tee.

The tenth fairway was now open. This hole is a par-4 dogleg right. A long drive with a fade would shorten the hole, but there was a deep bunker where the fairway turned right, and left of the fairway was a growth of lentil plants. Dick was on the tee. He chose a 3-wood to drive. This avoided hitting into the bunker on the right or running through the fairway into the lentils. His drive faded slightly but fell short of the bunker.

Phogg-Smythe and Halestork conferred briefly before Phogg-Smythe pulled his driver from the bag. I had noted on the practice range that he could hit the ball some 260 yards but tended to slice. He addressed the ball, and with his characteristic loop in his backswing, he sent the ball in a long, slicing arc into the deep bunker. Halestork started walking toward the bunker as soon as his partner drove the ball, sensing it would find the sand.

Dick and the doctor walked to where Dick's drive landed. The doctor selected a midiron, glanced at the bunker to make sure he was away, and lofted a shot that landed softly on the green about twelve feet from the flagstick. Halestork was next to hit. I watched him enter the bunker, and after several practice swings, he blasted a shot to about fifty yards short of the green. Phogg-Smythe played an excellent pitch shot to just a few feet from the cup. Now on the green, Dick had a putt for birdie. It was downhill, and he nudged it to about a foot from the cup. This putt was conceded. Halestork now had a short putt for par, which he sank.

The difficult eleventh hole, a 212-yard par-3, was halved with bogies. Both pros missed the green with their tee shots, and the writers played poor chip shots, leaving their partners with long putts, which they failed to get down in par.

The twelfth hole, a par-4, presented a birdie opportunity. Dick was the first to hit. The doctor indicated the tee shot should be aimed down the left side of the fairway so the second shot didn't cross the deep bunker to the right of the green. Dick nodded his approval and teed off with a 3-wood that landed in the left-center of the fairway, leaving the doctor with a short-iron shot to the green.

Phogg-Smythe stepped to the tee and smashed a drive of some 260 yards down the right-center of the fairway. For their second shots, the doctor lofted an 8-iron that landed in the middle of the green. Halestork then followed with a wedge that flew over the bunker and landed some twenty feet from the flag. This left Phogg-Smythe with a downhill putt. He barely tapped the ball, and it trickled slowly toward the cup, stopping a foot short. Now it was Dick's putt. The doctor pointed about an inch outside the left lip of the hole as an aiming point. Dick followed the doctor's advice and stroked a putt that first seemed too far left before it broke right and sank for a birdie. He and the doctor were now 4-up.

The short thirteenth hole, a par-3, was halved with par. Both writers missed makeable birdie putts.

Approaching the fourteenth tee, I saw several members of a search group inspecting the wreckage of the V-1 now that it was low tide. One member was wearing rubber waders and a face mask. He entered the water and briefly submerged for about twenty seconds. When he emerged, he removed the face mask and spoke briefly to his associates before the group walked to where Grafton was waiting for them in the jeep. The man who had worn the face mask removed the waders, climbed onto the jeep with the others, and off they went. I assumed we would find out more about the explosion when we finished the round.

Meanwhile, on fourteen, Dick had teed off and sliced his drive into the mustard. Phogg-Smythe then stepped on the tee, and after several vigorous practice swings, he powered a drive down the left-center of the fairway. The doctor retrieved Dick's drive from the mustard and dropped the ball in the rough beside the mustard. Because this was a par-5 hole, he attempted with a 3-wood but smothered the shot, advancing the ball about one hundred yards. The next shot was Halestork's. He hammered a 3-wood that stopped just short of the green. Dick now had a 3-wood of some 250 yards to the green that he struck well, but it came ten yards short of the green. The doctor now had a chip shot that he stroked to about five feet from the cup. Phogg-Smythe now had a short pitch shot. He stroked a shot to about two feet from the cup. Dick now had a five-foot putt that broke right to left. He failed to play enough break, and with that, they conceded their opponent's short putt. Dick and the doctor were now 3-up.

The short fifteenth hole was halved with par, and it was on to the sixteenth, a 400-yard par-4. The match was now dormie. Phogg-Smythe led off with a drive that sliced into a bunker in the middle of a potato patch. Dick followed with a drive of some 230 yards down the middle. Halestork had the next shot. He descended into the bunker and attempted to hit a short-iron out, but the ball caught the lip of the bunker and advanced only about fifty yards down the fairway. The doctor then struck a 6-iron to the green that landed beyond the flag and backed up to about two feet from the cup. Phogg-Smythe needed a wedge shot that would land within par range. He struck a shot that passed over the flag, landed on the back edge of the green, and then trickled over the edge into the deep bunker behind the green that had been a bomb crater before being partially filled in. Halestork walked to the back of the green and glanced down at the bottom of the bunker before walking over to Dick and the doctor and conceding the hole and the match three and two.

Phogg-Smythe and Halestork offered their congratulations on the win and the excellent shots Dick and the doctor had played. Then we all walked back to the clubhouse where the other teams were relaxing. Sir Harold was in the clubhouse, and when he saw us, he asked for everyone's attention. He then announced that the police and Military Intelligence wanted to keep the findings related to the explosion confidential and not talk to anyone who might be curious about the event. However, if pressed for information by friends, we were to say we heard it was a naval mine that had hit the beach and nothing more. We all agreed to this and moved to the bar to unwind. We obtained beer, whiskey, or gin and moved to the veranda.

Waiting on the veranda was a member of Military Intelligence, Inspector Gillespie, who reiterated Sir Harold's message that we were not to reveal anything about the explosion or the body found on the links. If no mention was made about the body, whoever was involved would eventually file a missing person's report with Scotland Yard. Inspector Gillespie went on to say that the large tubular structure embedded in the shoreline was the jet engine, and it appeared to have been partially sawed from the mounting on the bomb. The attempt to remove it no doubt caused the explosion.

Someone on the veranda asked who would want it since there were several intact V-1 bombs that had been deactivated and kept in military museums. Cyril Popinjay piped up and said there are scavengers who seek any sort of military hardware to sell on a black market for such things.

46

The inspector expanded further about who might want a V-1 or part of it. There are foreign governments that seek military equipment from other countries. Whoever was attempting to dislodge the V-1 from the shore may have thought because it hadn't exploded after all these years, it was safe to remove it. And perhaps it was only the engine that was of value. Attempting to remove the entire bomb would require the services of a marine salvage company. If removed from the shore, it would probably be towed to where it could be placed on a truck and taken to where it could be smuggled out to whomever paid for it. All very complicated. The best guess was that it was the engine and perhaps the guidance system that was of value. He concluded his remarks by again stressing the importance of not revealing anything about the explosion. He then excused himself and left with Sir Harold.

The golfers returned to the clubhouse for another round of drinks before walking back to the veranda to discuss what they had just heard. Several of us noted a figure practicing on the range; it was Miss Shotwell. She was hitting a 9-iron or wedge to Grafton who barely had to move to retrieve the balls. It was a pleasure to watch her: so accurate, so smooth, so rhythmic. Bumbry exclaimed her swing looked too hard for him to copy. Cloverjoy disagreed and told Bumbry that if he watched her long enough, he might learn something about the golf swing. Soon, she finished practice and signaled Grafton to return with her practice bag.

Dr. Middlefield had been watching her and quickly went to his golf bag and returned with a handful of golf balls. He met Miss Shotwell as she was about to leave the range. They chatted for a few minutes before he gave her his driver and teed up a ball. After several practice swings, she belted a drive of at least 250 yards. She hit two more similar drives before returning the driver to the doctor. When they returned to the clubhouse, he revealed he was using the new Wilcox Jubilee ball, which he said traveled at least ten to fifteen yards farther than current balls on the market. There was a limited distribution of these, but he promised he would obtain several dozen for her. Grafton retrieved the balls from the range since they were too valuable to be left there.

Miss Shotwell returned to the range to pick up a jacket she had worn when she started practice. As she started to return, she uttered a scream not unlike the one when she saw the arm in the bunker. Those of us who had returned to the veranda heard the scream and sensed something was wrong. We ran to the range where she pointed in the direction of the tomato growth along the eighteenth fairway. Dr. Middlefield took her arm and escorted her back to the clubhouse. He told us she had muttered to him that there was a body part at the edge of the tomatoes. She was breathing rapidly as she sat down in a chair. Dick went to the bar and obtained a cold, wet towel for her to hold to her face. We didn't question her further as she appeared too distressed to explain to us what had triggered her scream.

Grafton was in the clubhouse and immediately phoned Excelsior House to inform Sir Harold about Miss Shotwell's discovery.

Leffingwell and Sir Harold arrived and, on being informed about the site of Miss Shotwell's discovery, sped off to examine the area. Meanwhile, the doctor had ordered two gin and tonics, one for himself and one for Miss Shotwell. He told her the quinine would help settle her nerves. She eyed the drink suspiciously at first and then took a sip. The doctor took a big gulp from his drink. She then took a second sip and said it was quite refreshing. A few minutes later, Sir Harold and Leffingwell returned and said they would notify the police about a suspicious finding in the tomatoes. Meanwhile, no one was to search the area by the tomatoes.

Sir Harold said to Miss Shotwell that he would drive her to Excelsior House, but she said she was feeling better and would have another gin and tonic. Sir Harold eyed her empty glass but didn't say anything. Then he and Leffingwell left for Excelsior House to notify the police.

Several sportswriters, notebooks in hand, asked Miss Shotwell if she remembered what she had seen. Dick quickly intervened and said he was sure she didn't want to recall such an unsettling finding, and he reminded the writers they were not to reveal anything about the explosion or body. With that, the notebooks were returned to their pockets. After a few minutes, Dr. Middlefield and Miss Shotwell finished their drinks, and the doctor said he would drive Miss Shotwell to Excelsior House. The rest of us decided we would return to the Prince Rupert Hotel.

Back at the Prince Rupert, we all headed for the Bunch of Carrots for another round of beverages. Geoff Cloverjoy was the first to speak up and asked what we thought Miss Shotwell saw that upset her. Ian Crankshaw and Mel Camberwick both suspected it was another body part, possibly the head of the victim. We all agreed whatever she saw must have been frightening. Dick then wondered if the matches would be played tomorrow because law enforcement may want to close Gnomewood Links and make a thorough search for any other missing body parts. Crankshaw said we probably won't find out until tomorrow if or when we will play.

Talk then turned to the matches just completed and who would be competing tomorrow, assuming play would continue. Frogwell-Potts and Nippengay were winners and would tee off against Popinjay and Sapwood. Crankshaw and Feathershanks would face the defending champions, Camberwick and Quickfoot. And in the last match, Phogg-Smythe and Halestork would face Whistle and Middlefield.

Some criticism of the links followed. Camberwick said, partly in jest, that he was sure the vegetables attracted golf balls. This brought a few laughs. The sixth hole came in for more complaints. The elephant grass on the left of the dogleg and the carrots on the right made the hole too penal. Someone exclaimed, "Try hitting the fairway." Frogwell-Potts said the tee should be moved up on the 212-yard eleventh hole. His pro partner, Nippengay, told him that hitting into the prevailing wind made a long-iron shot particularly difficult. The iron was usually short, and a 3-wood was too much club. Camberwick suggested letting the pros decide about the length of eleven since they were usually the ones hitting first. Maybe they should consider carrying a 5-wood for this hole. The discussion ended when the aroma of food drifted into the Bunch of Carrots, and the group decided it was time for dinner.

The featured dish on the menu was a meat pie consisting of chicken, potatoes, carrots, and mushrooms. Accompanying this was a rather immature Chablis. Talk at dinner centered around the effects of the war on certain courses. For example, Turnberry had been turned into an airfield, and the hotel associated with the links became a hospital. The links has since been renovated and has now been considered suitable for a major championship. Some courses, Rye for example, had defense positions dug in, fearing an invasion early in the war. The links has since been returned to its role as the site of the President's Putter, the competition between the Oxford and Cambridge Golf Societies. Dick pointed out here at Gnomewood, the links suffered damage from German bombs and strafing by fighter planes. Fortunately, Sir Harold had the damage to the links and the clubhouse repaired so that, by 1947, the course was playable.

Several young sports reporters who happened to be dining at the Prince Rupert moved their chairs closer to our table to share our conversation. They had some experience in reporting on golf and were eager to hear more about the craft. Ian Crankshaw told them they should get to know the players—even if their first interview was short. The golfers would get to know them and, hopefully, respect their impression of their play in a tournament. Dick suggested they should read Bernard Darwin's columns in the *Times* and his book on golf course design. These sources could help the young writers better understand tournament competition and the stage on which a golf performance was being played.

Byf Barleycroft entered the dining room after settling some wagers at the Foggy Shores. He said he thought the food was better at Prince Rupert, but after looking at the menu, he decided he would return to his fellow pros at Foggy Shores and dine there. As he was leaving, he looked at our table and said he wanted assurances there would be accurate reporting of his match today, defeating Bumbry and Dedmon.

Dick replied, "Of course, just like always. I'll make a point of embellishing your stellar play."

With that good-natured exchange, Byf departed for the Foggy Shores.

I asked Dick why the sportswriters and professionals stayed at separate hotels. He said he had heard that in the first few tournaments, all the contestants stayed at the Prince Rupert, but arguments would break out between writers and pros. On at least one occasion, a team accused the other of cheating—and they nearly came to blows. Sir Harold thought it best to keep the pros and writers separate.

After dinner and dessert, we adjourned to the Bunch of Carrots to enjoy brandy and a cigar. Crankshaw had whiskey. Soon, a pleasant fatigue settled over me, and I excused myself and headed for bed. The others said they would finish their brandies and depart shortly for their rooms. They needed sleep for tomorrow's matches.

CHAPTER 6

Sunlight flooded my room around six. I had forgotten to pull the shades before going to bed. I glanced out the window to see what people on the street were wearing. A light sweater seemed adequate. After dressing, I sat down at a small table in my room and composed some notes about what had transpired yesterday.

After about an hour, I put the notes in a folder containing material I had written since I arrived at Gnomewood and headed down to breakfast. I joined Dick, Ian Crankshaw, and Phil Frogwell-Potts. On the table were a large bowl of fruit, hot buns, bacon, and a large pot of tea. Conversation was at a minimum as the players anticipated the day's competition. The only chatter came from several sportswriters who were covering the tournament for their respective newspapers.

Shortly after eight thirty, the bus took us to the clubhouse. As we were getting off the bus, I noted several horse trailers parked near the clubhouse. The horses were being unloaded by men wearing red jodhpurs, blue jackets, and white sun helmets. Dick recognized the uniforms and explained the men and horses were under the direction of retired Major Laurence Spavins and were a cavalry demonstration troop that performed at county fairs and on certain holidays.

After being saddled, a dozen horses were led to the area around the first tee where they were mounted. Sir Harold and a constable drove up in the jeep and welcomed Major Spavins. They spoke briefly before Sir Harold returned to the jeep and the major mounted his horse. After looking over the men and horses, the major blew a whistle twice, and the line moved slowly forward, each horse being separated by about ten yards. I immediately recognized the horse troop was inspecting Gnomewood

Links for body parts in the aftermath of the explosion. Sir Harold and the constable followed the line of horses in the jeep.

As we were watching, Leffingwell approached us and said the semifinal matches would start around ten thirty. Consequently, I estimated that following the semifinal matches, the final match probably wouldn't start until two. The four players in the first match—Cloverjoy, Barleycroft, Frogwell-Potts, and Nippengay—upon being informed of the starting time, decided to take their clubs to the practice range to warm up. The two Scotsmen, who were playing in the second match against Dick and doctor Middlefield, decided to return to the clubhouse. Dick and I followed them. The doctor had not yet arrived.

Outside the clubhouse, Leffingwell watched the progress of the horsemen and advised that when the line of horses reached the ninth hole and turned back toward the clubhouse, the players should start practice. The Scotsmen agreed with this plan. Dick hoped the doctor would arrive soon. We chatted for a while, and then Feathershanks suggested a putting contest. Just as they were about to start, the doctor came roaring up to the clubhouse parking lot. He emerged with his clubs and noted the horse trailers, asking if an equestrian event was being held before the tournament.

Dick informed him that the horse troop was inspecting the links for evidence linked to the explosion, and the players were about to start a putting contest. The doctor thought this was an excellent idea and pulled his putter from his golf bag. As the putting progressed, I noted a figure in a skirt approaching. It was Miss Shotwell carrying her golf bag. I interrupted the putting and asked if they would mind if she joined them. I assumed she would. They all agreed she could join them provided she add one pound to the purse. I said I would stake her "entrance fee."

It didn't take long before she had won two holes and was threatening the leader, Colin Feathershanks, for the lead. As the players were finishing the first round of the putting contest, Leffingwell drove up and announced the line of horsemen had finished inspecting the front nine and were starting on the back nine. Dick responded that they should start practice and agreed that Feathershanks be declared the winner.

On the practice range, Cloverjoy and Barleycroft were preparing to face Frogwell-Potts and Nippengay in the first match. After practicing for about ten minutes, Cloverjoy walked over to Miss Shotwell, who was watching the group warm up, and offered to let her hit a few shots with his driver. She hesitated and then accepted his offer. Rather than use the practice balls, she took a ball from her pocket, teed it up, and blasted a drive of at least 250 yards. She repeated this with a second ball. Cloverjoy was amazed. He asked her where she had obtained these two balls, and she said Dr. Middlefield had given them to her as a gift. She declined to hit any more golf balls because she said Cloverjoy's driver didn't fit her swing. Cloverjoy then speculated that she would probably gain even more distance using her own driver. She and Cloverjoy chatted for a few minutes about upcoming matches, and she handed back his driver. He rejoined Barleycroft.

Dick noticed the line of horses had reached the fifteenth fairway and speculated it would be another thirty minutes before the horsemen completed their sweep of the links. After Dr. Middlefield finished hitting a few drives, he had Dick practice hitting a few 3-wood shots with the Jubilee ball and then switching to his 3-iron to see the difference in distance. The 3-wood produced at least twenty or thirty yards more distance. The distance wasn't as great using the ball they had used yesterday, the Dunlap Avenger, which the doctor thought had better wind penetration characteristics. Using his driver, Dick was convinced the Jubilee was at least ten to fifteen yards longer. They agreed to play the Jubilee ball.

The two Scotsmen had finished practice and announced they were returning to the clubhouse for refreshments. Dick and the doctor followed but paused briefly to watch the horsemen advancing down the eighteenth fairway. The doctor estimated the tournament would start in about half an hour, and they went to the clubhouse to grab a quick lunch. Inside, the Scotsmen were having beer and cheese sandwiches. Dick and the doctor had sausage sandwiches and cider. Players in the other match were having beer along with cheese sandwiches. As they were eating, a police van passed by the clubhouse window. It stopped nearby and a constable deposited a black plastic bag obtained from one of the horsemen into the van. Sir Harold and Leffingwell drove up in the jeep and, after they spoke briefly with Major Spavins, the major blew a whistle. The men dismounted and led their horses to the trailers. After the horses were led into the trailers, the major climbed into the lead truck and waved goodbye to Sir Harold as the trucks and trailers started down the road.

The players finished lunch and decided to return to the putting green for some last-minute practice. However, Barleycroft and Cloverjoy decided to move to the first tee, although the start had not yet been announced. Just then, Sir Harold, Leffingwell, and the announcer, Harley Bellows, drove up to the first tee. This was Dick's signal to return his putter in his golf bag and walk to the first tee.

A few individuals in the gallery applauded the appearance of the golfers. They had, no doubt, been entertained by the horse troop, but their attention was now focused on the start of the tournament. The eight golfers gathered around the first tee made a colorful scene. There were Byford Barleycroft in his bright red slacks, Geoff Cloverjoy in green slacks and yellow sweater, Frogwell-Potts in dark blue slacks and blue-and-white striped golf shirt, Giles Nippengay in red-and-white checkered slacks, Colin Feathershanks in dark red plus fours with red, white, and blue stockings, Dr. Middlefield in white plus fours with black-and-white checkered stockings, and, finally, Dick in dark gray slacks and light blue sweater.

I looked at the spectators to see if Miss Shotwell was present. She was standing by Sir Harold's wife, Dorothy, sipping tea. I walked over to where they were standing and told Mrs. Gilroy how much I enjoyed watching the professionals and sportswriters compete. I asked if they were going to follow the matches this morning. Mrs. Gilroy replied that she and Miss Shotwell were going to return to Excelsior House and return for the championship match in the afternoon. I commented on the excellent condition of the course, particularly after last night's storm, and she said they were fortunate to have Leffingwell and Grafton working at Gnomewood Links.

I excused myself when I heard the thundering voice of Harley Bellows announcing the start of the day's competition. On the tee were Barleycroft and Cloverjoy and their opponents, Frogwell-Potts and Nippengay. Finbarr Slattery was now caddying for Nippengay. Among the spectators was Barleycroft's brother Hylton, who was on the winning team in 1937. Bellows pointed him out to the spectators, and Hylton waved to the gallery. Following that, Nippengay stepped to the teeing area and teed up his ball. After two practice swings, he belted a drive of 250 yards. Next up was Barleycroft. He took one whiplike practice swing and hammered a drive of at least 270 yards. Generous applause followed these drives.

As the players from this first match strode down the fairway, Dick and the doctor, along with Crankshaw and Feathershanks, left the putting green and walked to the first tee. During the warm-up earlier, I had noticed Feathershanks using a shiny walnut-colored driver with a red and white face insert. When he had paused between practice swings, I asked if the driver was new. He replied it was a new "born-in-Scotland" driver he had just obtained from a small company in Dundee, and he had just put it in play. I wondered if he had gotten the feel of the club yet, but I noted he was hitting the ball straight and didn't question him about using it in this tournament.

The other semifinalists were on the tee, and they shook hands and inspected each other's golf balls. Feathershanks remarked he had heard of the Jubilee ball the doctor would be using to tee off but hadn't obtained any yet because he played the Dunlap 66 ball, and he and his partner would use it today. The Scotsmen had won the coin toss, and as Feathershanks teed up his ball, Harley Bellows introduced him as a recent winner of the Outer Hebrides Open. Feathershanks took one practice swing and belted a drive of some 270 yards.

As Dr. Carrington Middlefield approached the tee, Bellows said, "The most successful golfing dentist in Great Britain."

This brought a laugh from the gallery.

The doctor tipped his visor to the gallery and then slammed a drive of close to 280 yards. I was impressed by the length of these drives and realized neither team would have an advantage in driving length.

Rather than follow the match through the front nine, I wanted to conserve my strength for the closing holes and decided to return to the clubhouse. Miss Shotwell and Mrs. Gilroy were finishing tea. I asked Miss Shotwell if she would be practicing this morning and mentioned that I would be glad to shag practice balls for her. I assumed Leffingwell and Grafton would be concentrating their efforts on the tournament.

Miss Shotwell said, "Yes, as soon as I finish my tea."

Mrs. Gilroy said she was returning to Excelsior House and told us to take advantage of the opportunity to practice. Miss Shotwell finished her tea and then took her clubs from her locker. I grabbed a bag of practice balls, and we were off to the range.

I walked out to the 100-yard mark, and Miss Shotwell proceeded to hit a short-iron that landed near my feet. I moved back progressively. Finally, I moved from 200 yards to the 250-yard mark. I saw her take several balls from her golf bag rather than from the practice ball bag. This indicated she was going to hit the Jubilee balls Dr. Middlefield had given her. She proceeded to hit these between 230 and 240 yards. I was amazed at the ease of her swing and the distance she was achieving. Back in the States, the only woman golfer I had witnessed who could hit a golf ball more than 250 yards was the "Babe." I put these balls in my pocket so they wouldn't be mixed with the practice balls. When she had hit the last of these Jubilee balls, two of which did reach the 250-yard mark, she motioned for me to return to the base of the range.

Miss Shotwell and I walked back to the clubhouse, had a soft drink, and relaxed on the veranda. I asked her what her future plans were. Was she planning on qualifying for the British Women's Amateur or for the Women's Open? Did she have any thoughts about competing in America? I told her I thought her game was good enough to compete in our US Women's Amateur. She said she hoped to qualify for the British Women's Amateur. I said I would be glad to caddie for her, but my job would interfere with her golf schedule. She thanked me and said her father would be her caddie if she qualified for the Women's Amateur. Driving up to the clubhouse was Soufflé in the motorcycle. He said he was to pick up Miss Shotwell and drive her back to Excelsior House. She said she would see me later this afternoon.

I was about to venture out on the links when an elderly gentleman wearing blue plus fours and a bright yellow sweater approached and asked if I would join him on the veranda. I hesitated for a second, not sure what to make of this invitation, but I said I could spare a few minutes. He might be a friend of Sir Harold's. I asked if he would like a ginger ale, and he thanked me for this offering. We took our beverages out to the veranda, and he introduced himself as Leslie Goodspeed. I introduced myself, and he immediately recognized I was from the States and asked how I had heard of the Gnomewood tournament. I told him I had heard about the tournament from my friend and sportswriter Dick Whistle. He filled his pipe and proceeded to tell me something about the history of the tournament at Gnomewood Links. The tournament had initially been called Pros and Poets, but too many poets rather than sportswriters showed up to play so the tournament became "Golf among the Vegetables." From the beginning, Sir Harold Gilroy had instituted the rule than only seven clubs could be used. He then began to describe in some detail the various areas in which vegetables had grown. At this point, I was beginning to feel like a golfer in a P. G. Wodehouse story trapped by the "oldest member" and compelled to listen to one of his stories. He went on; the practice range had once been devoted to nothing but carrots. Celery and cucumbers were grown on what are now the seventh and eighth holes. Potatoes were grown on sixteen and the eighteenth fairway. I realized he could probably talk for hours about reseeding the fairways, and I was eager to return to the tournament. I saw the red slacks of Barleycroft and told Leslie that I wanted to see more of the matches. As I rose to leave, I said I would see him later, but I never did.

I caught up with the players on the sixth hole. Cloverjoy had hit a wavering drive, and Barleycroft was judging what club to use next. His caddie, Knutty Baldridge, was throwing grass clippings in the air to try to determine the wind direction. Barleycroft, satisfied he had the wind at his back, then lofted a midiron to about ten feet from the flagstick.

Next to hit was Nippengay. His partner, Frogwell-Potts, had driven into the carrots, and Nippengay had taken a drop outside the carrots. From this spot, he hit a 3-iron to the back of the green that rolled onto the short grass surrounding the green. Frogwell-Potts was now away. Nippengay advised him to use his putter rather than wedge to chip. This he did, and he rolled a putt to about a foot from the cup. This putt was conceded. Now it was Cloverjoy's turn to putt. He stroked a putt to the right lip of the cup and the tap-in was conceded. The hole was halved, and according to a spectator, the match was even.

Looking back at the sixth tee, I saw Crankshaw ready to hit. Feathershanks was pointing to the right, indicating where to aim, but Crankshaw drove directly to the left and into the elephant grass. I'd made this mistake in the past when playing golf. Dick was now up. I assumed he would aim his drive to the right, and he did. His drive landed in the carrots. Crankshaw and Feathershanks decided to hit a provisional ball, assuming the drive into the elephant grass was lost or unplayable. They searched for the ball for at least five minutes before declaring a lost ball and deciding to play the provisional ball, which had landed in the rough.

The doctor found Dick's drive in the carrots and, after finding the ball, played a shot from the rough to about twelve feet from the flag. Feathershanks had hit the provisional drive, and Crankshaw now had a shot from the rough. He took several practice swings and blasted the ball out to just short of the green. Feathershanks played their fifth shot to just short of the flag. Dick's birdie putt just missed the cup, and Feathershanks picked up their ball, conceding the hole. Dick and the doctor were now 1-up.

The seventh hole was halved with bogies and the short eighth with pars. The ninth hole was a 525-yard par-5. The breeze was partly in the players' faces. The doctor was on the tee, and he hammered a 270-yard drive that drifted to the edge of the eggplants. Feathershanks, eager to show off his new driver, blasted a slightly longer drive, but it rolled into a fairway bunker on the left. Crankshaw entered the bunker, and he and Feathershanks conferred before Crankshaw blasted out with a short-iron. The ball landed in the fairway about one hundred yards from the green. Feathershanks then played a wedge to about fifteen feet from the flag. Meanwhile, Dick had played a 3-wood to just short of the green, and the doctor then chipped to about five feet from the cup. Both writers now had birdie putts, Dick's being much shorter. Crankshaw's putt came up short, and the remaining putt was conceded. The doctor pointed to the right lip of the cup as an aiming point for Dick. He took several practice strokes, lined up the putt, and sank it. There was scattered applause from the gallery. He and the doctor were now 2-up.

In the refreshment area between nine and ten, three of the players had soft drinks and sandwiches. The doctor had a beer and large pretzel. A few spectators were lingering in the refreshment area, and I asked them who was leading in the first match. They told me Barleycroft and Cloverjoy were 2-up—and Barleycroft was driving exceptionally well. Frogwell-Potts and Nippengay were lucky to be only 2-down.

The tenth hole was halved with par. The difficult 212-yard par-3 was halved with bogies. Both pros missed the green with 3-irons, and the writers hit timid chip shots, resulting in long par putts that the pros failed to sink.

The twelfth hole, a 365-yard par-4, played downwind. On the tee, Dick and the doctor discussed club choice. The doctor pulled the 3-wood from Dick's bag and said this was enough club. There were parsley patches on both sides of the fairway, and the rough outside the parsley was particularly thick. Dick responded by using his 3-wood off the tee and stroked a 220-yard shot in the fairway. The Scotsmen then held a brief conference and decided this was a birdie hole. Consequently, Crankshaw used his driver and belted a 250-yard shot down the middle, leaving Feathershanks with an easy wedge shot to the green. The doctor then played Dick's drive with an 8-iron to about ten feet from the flagstick. Feathershanks then stroked a wedge to about six feet from the flag. Now it was up to the writers to sink their birdie putts. Dick and the doctor looked over Dick's putt and decided there was a slight left-to-right break. Dick lined up the putt and stroked a good putt that barely missed on the right. Crankshaw saw his chance for a birdie, got down on his hands and knees, and tried to decide if there was any break in the six-foot putt. He then took his stance, and after two practice strokes, he putted on-line to the hole, but the putt stopped an inch from the cup. Both remaining short putts were conceded. Crankshaw muttered something to his partner in a dialect I couldn't understand. As we moved on to the next hole, Dick murmured to me, "We dodged a bullet on this hole."

The 145-yard thirteenth hole was deceptively difficult. Although the hole is relatively short, the green slopes from left to right and is guarded by two bunkers on the right and a deep bunker behind. The doctor was first to hit. He lofted a gentle fade with an 8-iron that stopped about twelve feet below and to the right of the flag. Feathershanks followed with a crisp 8-iron that flew over the flag and landed on the back edge of the green before rolling down into the deep bunker. The ball was sitting up as Crankshaw entered the bunker.

Dick and I walked to the edge of the bunker and saw that Crankshaw should be able to blast out relatively easily. The difficulty would be in stopping the ball near the hole. Feathershanks stood by the edge of the green and coached his partner to open the blade and give it a "good rip." After several practice swings, Feathershanks exploded the ball out in a fog of sand, the ball landing about twenty feet below the hole.

Not bad, I thought. *This gives them a chance at par.*

Feathershanks was first to putt. He stroked a good putt that just missed the edge of the hole. The remaining putt was conceded. Dick now had the birdie putt that the doctor cautioned to lag and not go for the hole since par would win. Dick followed this advice and putted to about a foot from the hole. This was conceded, and he and the doctor were now 3-up.

The fourteenth hole was a 517-yard par-5 dogleg left. The tee shot was into the prevailing wind. Dick was on the tee, and his wavering shot landed just to the right of the mustard. Crankshaw's drive was twenty yards farther and in the fairway. The doctor slammed a 3-wood across the dogleg that landed in a left bunker just short of the green. Feathershanks was next to hit, and he drilled a 3-wood that also landed in a bunker short of the green, on the right. Both writers now had bunker shots that offered a chance for setting up a birdie putt. Dick was away and played a shot that landed about fifteen feet from the flag. Crankshaw then blasted out to about ten feet from the flag. Both pros missed the birdie putts, and the short putts were conceded.

On the fifteenth hole, a par-3, the match involving Frogwell-Potts and Nippengay against Cloverjoy and Barleycroft was still in progress. Frogwell-Potts was in the rough beside the pea patch. He lofted a shot that landed about twenty feet from the flag. Barleycroft's tee shot landed about six feet from the cup. Nippengay had to sink the twenty-footer to save par. His putt just missed. He looked at the six-foot putt his opponents had for birdie and decided they would at least make par and conceded the hole. Barleycroft and Cloverjoy were now 3-up.

After pacing back and forth on the tee, the doctor was ready to hit. He stroked a 6-iron to about eight feet from the flagstick. Feathershanks then matched the doctor's tee shot by hitting to about six feet from the flag. The two writers now had birdie putts. Dick was slightly away, and his putt failed on the right—and Crankshaw's putt ended up just short. The match was now dormie.

The sixteenth hole was a 400-yard par-4 playing downwind. There was a sizable potato growth along the fairway on the right in the middle of which was a deep bunker, the result of a German bomb. On the tee, following the doctor's advice, Dick selected a 3-wood to drive and smacked a shot of 240 yards. Crankshaw used his driver to blast a shot of at least 260 yards. These drives left their partners with short-iron shots to the green. The doctor and then Feathershanks lofted shots that landed seven to eight feet from the flag. Crankshaw was away. He and Feathershanks lined up the putt before Crankshaw took his stance, took two practice swings, and rolled in the putt for a birdie. Now the pressure was on Dick. His putt was seven feet straight uphill. He took several practice strokes, lined up the putt, and stroked it into the cup. They won three and two and were in the finals!

The doctor rushed up to congratulate Dick, followed by their opponents. Dick had a look of relief as his half smile became a full grin. The gallery applauded as the players turned to walk back to the clubhouse. Ahead of them were Cloverjoy and Barleycroft. I assumed they had won since well-wishers were patting Barleycroft on the back.

Back at the clubhouse, Barleycroft was enjoying a victory cigar on the veranda. As we passed, he exclaimed, "Cloverjoy and I are looking forward to our match this afternoon."

Dick and the doctor paused, nodded in agreement, and entered the clubhouse. Some of the gallery had joined Barleycroft on the veranda. The doctor suggested he and Dick stay in the clubhouse and relax there. Inside, the doctor's wife, Edith, gave him a small bag containing a change of clothes. Dick had left a clean shirt in his locker, and he and the doctor changed into their afternoon attire. The doctor now wore dark gray plus fours, light gray stockings, and a red golf shirt. He retained his white visor. Dick changed into a bright yellow golf shirt.

The doctor, Edith, Dick, and I sat down at a table and ordered Berkshire sausage sandwiches. We all chose cider to accompany these choices. We ate in relative silence, with Dick commenting on the excellent quality of the sausage. Edith asked her husband if he had his pills, and he muttered, "Yes, they are somewhere." There was no further conversation.

When we finished lunch, the doctor said we should head for the practice range at about one thirty. He looked around the clubhouse and saw two comfortable-looking leather chairs, perfect for a nap. Dick and the doctor settled in the chairs, and Edith and I remained at the table and chatted about upcoming tournaments. She knew her husband looked forward to qualifying for the Open at St. Andrews and competing against golfers such as Bobby Locke and Peter Thompson. I said I hoped to cover the Open but might have another assignment at home when the Open would be played.

The two Scotsmen came by our table and wished the doctor and Dick good luck. They had been talking to Barleycroft who they said expressed great confidence that he and Cloverjoy would be winners. Dick and the doctor had been dozing, and I don't know if they heard about Barleycroft's boast. If they did, I don't think the two needed any extra motivation to play their best.

CHAPTER 7

At one thirty, Sir Harold came through the clubhouse and announced the final match would begin at two o'clock. The caddies, Bobby Clambourne and Knutty Baldridge, whom Dick had hired as his caddie, were already on the practice range There was a gallery of perhaps one hundred people gathered by the range to watch the players warming up. The doctor started practicing with his short irons and then progressed to his 6-iron, then his 3-iron, and finally his driver. He was hitting at twice the pace of Dick, who was more methodical in his warm-up. The doctor had given Dick a few of the Jubilee balls to use to judge the extra distance they would provide. They finished practice on the range and moved over to the practice putting green. Barleycroft and Cloverjoy were already testing the speed of the green. The doctor told Dick that the greens would be faster this afternoon because the sun and breeze had dried them.

Cloverjoy and Barleycroft finished putting and walked to the first tee. Barleycroft's fans were offering encouragement, and Dick and the doctor finished putting and followed their opponents to the first tee. The doctor received modest applause from his fans who followed his play on the professional circuit.

On the tee, the two teams shook hands. I heard Barleycroft praising the doctor and expressing hope that he and Cloverjoy would make a good showing against such formidable opponents. The doctor smiled at this gamesmanship.

Sir Harold stepped forward with a cap containing two golf balls numbered 1 and 2 and asked Dick and Cloverjoy to draw from the cap. I thought, *If Cloverjoy draws number one and Barleycroft tees off first, there could be a repeat of day one when Barleycroft drove out of bounds and a nervous Cloverjoy whiffed on their next shot.* Instead, Dick picked the ball marked 1.

The booming voice of Harley Bellows flooded the air as he announced, "On the tee, Dr. Carrington Middlefield, recent winner of the Southland-on-Sea Open."

Moderate applause greeted the introduction as the doctor tipped his visor to the spectators and then proceeded to blast a 270-yard drive down the middle. As the doctor stepped back, he drifted over to where his wife was standing. I saw her slip a small pill bottle into his hand. I later found out the pills were Dexedrine, a relatively new stimulant. I didn't think he needed any more stimulation after that drive.

Harley Bellows then announced, "On the tee, from the Eastbourne Club, a renowned teacher and tournament player, Mr. Byford Barleycroft. His brother Hylton is here today. Hylton was a winner here in 1938. Please step forward, Hylton."

Generous applause greeted this introduction, and a spectator in a blue blazer stepped forward from the crowd. More applause followed. Barleycroft then teed up his ball and struck a long, fading drive that landed in the artichokes. A smattering of applause accompanied the golfers as they left the tee.

Cloverjoy found their ball in the artichokes and dropped it in the rough beside the artichokes. I walked over to the rough and saw the next shot from the rough would be difficult. Barleycroft's caddie handed Cloverjoy a 6-iron for his next shot. After several practice swings, he drilled a low-flying shot that landed in a bunker guarding the right side of the green. Dick had the next shot. He struck an 8-iron to about fifteen feet from the flagstick. Now it was Barleycroft's shot. From the bunker, he lofted a shot to about five feet from the flag. Cloverjoy would have a five-footer for par. Next to play was the doctor. He struck a good putt that just missed the cup on the left edge. The tap-in was conceded. Cloverjoy now had the five-foot putt to tie. He and Barleycroft surveyed the line. It appeared there was a slight right-to-left break. Cloverjoy then took his stance, took one practice stroke, and tapped a putt that stopped on the lip. After a minute or so, the ball failed to drop, resulting in a bogie and loss of the hole. Dick and the doctor were 1-up.

The second hole, a par-4, was halved, and it was on to the 503-yard third hole. The doctor was on the tee and blasted a long drive that faded into a beet field. Next up was Barleycroft. He hammered a 280-yard drive down the middle. Dick walked to the beet field where he found his partner's drive. He took a drop into the rough and elected to hit a 3-iron rather than a 3-wood from a less than ideal lie. His iron shot landed about fifty yards short of the green. Cloverjoy was now away. He slammed a 3-wood that landed short of the green and rolled to about twenty feet from the flag. The doctor had a wedge shot of fifty yards that he lofted to about ten feet from the cup.

On the green, Barleycroft had a twenty-foot putt for an eagle. He lined it up and stroked a putt that just missed the right lip and rolled a foot beyond the cup. This remaining putt was conceded. Dick now had the ten-foot putt to tie their opponent's birdie. He and the doctor viewed the putt from all angles before Dick addressed the putt. After several practice strokes, he rolled a good putt that just missed, resulting in loss of the hole. The match was now even.

The match remained even until the difficult sixth hole. Cloverjoy's drive landed on the right edge of the fairway. Dick was aware of the danger of hitting into the elephant grass, but that's exactly what he did. The doctor wanted to hit a provisional ball, and Barleycroft wanted Dick to hit it. The doctor reminded Barleycroft that he had driven out of bounds in a previous match, and, in foursomes, the partner hits the next shot. Dr. Middlefield then teed up his ball, with no objection from Barleycroft, and belted a drive of some 270 yards down the right side of the fairway. Since the search through the elephant grass failed to uncover Dick's errant drive, Dick would play the provisional ball. He hit a 6-iron that landed in a bunker to the right of the green. The next shot was Barleycroft's. He struck a 6-iron to about ten feet from the flag. The doctor, in the bunker, then played their fourth shot to about six feet from the cup. Cloverjoy was next to play. He had the ten-foot putt for a birdie. His putt stopped a few inches short. The doctor picked up their opponent's ball, conceding the hole. Cloverjoy and Barleycroft were now 1-up.

The seventh and eighth holes were halved with par. The ninth hole was a 525-yard par-5, playing into a breeze. Barleycroft was on the tee, and he blasted a 250-yard drive down the middle. The doctor attempted to match Barleycroft's drive, but he hooked his shot into one of the bunkers along the left side of the fairway. This left Dick with a long bunker shot to the green. The bunker was deep enough that Dick could only play a 6-iron to the fairway.

The next shot was Cloverjoy's. He struck a beautiful 3-wood that landed about fifty yards short of the green. The doctor was now away. He played a wedge that hung up in the breeze and landed ten yards short of the green. A good chip and putt would give them par. Barleycroft now had a wedge shot of fifty yards that he struck to no more than three feet from the cup. Dick had a thirty-foot shot from off the green that he elected to play with his putter. I wasn't sure how well Dick had mastered using the putter from off the green, but he had seen this used enough times that he must have felt this was the best play. He stroked a good putt that stopped about five feet from the cup. The doctor had the five-footer to save par, and he sank it.

Cloverjoy now had the birdie putt to win the hole. He took several cautious practice strokes before lining up the putt. He stepped away briefly before lining it up again and stroking the ball to the lip where it hesitated before dropping. He and Barleycroft were now 2-up. Scattered applause greeted Barleycroft and Cloverjoy as they paused at the refreshment tent. Inside the tent were cheese sandwiches and cider or beer. The doctor's wife was waiting there, and I saw her give him a pill that he washed down with a big gulp of beer. Barleycroft and Cloverjoy opponents chose to wait outside the tent and mingle with the gallery. Inside, Dick and the doctor had sandwiches, one of which Dick gave me along with a bottle of cider. The doctor commented that the breeze had increased, which was to their advantage. Barleycroft usually played on inland courses, and playing in the wind might make judging distances difficult. He probably would ignore what club Cloverjoy might select.

Barleycroft and Cloverjoy were sitting on a bench outside the tent where they were conversing with well-wishers. Hylton Barleycroft was commenting on the quality of the competition thus far. I noted Byf had started a second beer. Perhaps he was accustomed to this refreshment during a round of golf, but I had played enough golf with my sportswriter colleagues to recognize how alcohol can have a negative effect on accuracy both in driving and on the greens. I hoped the doctor would limit himself to one beer.

Leffingwell and a young lady from the clubhouse drove up in the jeep and started to load the remaining sandwiches and beverages into the jeep. This was a signal to resume play.

Barleycroft stuck his head into the tent and asked, "Are you boys ready?"

The doctor told him they were ready.

Outside the tent, Cloverjoy had stepped to the tenth tee. He took two practice swings and launched a high slice into a bunker to the right of the fairway. The doctor told Dick to use his 3-wood because the wind was at their back, and distance wouldn't be a factor. Dick took several robust practice swings to loosen up and then smacked a drive of some 230 yards down the left-center of the fairway.

Barleycroft walked to the bunker where his partner's drive had landed. He saw he had a good lie and smacked a 6-iron to the edge of the green. The doctor had the next shot. He lofted an 8-iron that rode the breeze and landed about six feet from the flagstick. On the green, Cloverjoy had about a forty-foot putt over a rise and then down to the cup. He stroked a putt that stopped on the rise, leaving his partner with a ten-foot downhill putt for par. Barleycroft surveyed the downhill line before stepping up to putt. He boomed a putt that ran at least six feet beyond the cup. Dick was slightly away, and he putted to a few inches from the cup. At this point, Barleycroft conceded the hole. He and Cloverjoy were now 1-up.

Both teams bogeyed the 212-yard eleventh hole. The pros missed the green with their drives, as they did in the morning, and the writers hit poor chip shots that left long par putts that were missed. The relatively short par-4 twelfth hole of 365 yards presented a birdie opportunity. Dick had the honors. With the wind at his back, he struck a 3-wood that landed some 240 yards down the fairway. Barleycroft selected a 3-iron for Cloverjoy to hit off the tee.

I assumed that Cloverjoy's drive would be shorter and that Barleycroft would have the first shot to the green, often an advantage in match play. I had observed Cloverjoy on the practice range during the past few days and was not impressed with his ability with a long iron. As I suspected, he sliced his tee shot into the parsley.

The players, caddies, and a few spectators searched for several minutes before Barleycroft, whose shot it was, decided to play a shot from where he determined the ball had crossed the parsley. The doctor objected to this decision, pointing out that the ball may have bounced out of the parsley into the rough, and they should continue to search for a few more minutes. Barleycroft didn't agree to the doctor's objection and said he was going to take a drop between the parsley and the fairway.

I noted the rough was shorter where he planned to play his next shot.

Dick muttered something to the doctor before they agreed to Barleycroft's decision. Barleycroft dropped the ball in the short rough and hammed a 6-iron that the wind carried to the back of the green—and then over the edge into short grass.

The doctor walked to where Dick's drive had landed, took out an 8-iron, and hit a shot that landed about three feet from the flag. Cloverjoy had a chip shot that had to clear the back edge of the green before rolling downhill to the cup. He nervously gripped and regripped his wedge before stubbing his club behind the ball and advancing it only a few feet. Barleycroft now had a fifteen-foot downhill putt that he ran some five feet beyond the cup. The doctor reminded his opponents they were still away. Cloverjoy then putted to the edge of the cup. After a minute, Barleycroft conceded the hole. The match was now even.

The thirteenth hole was halved, and the teams moved on to the par-5 fourteenth hole. Dick was on the tee. The doctor pointed to the right side of the fairway and the adjacent mustard growth as the safe play, avoiding the three large bunkers on the left. Dick then struck a drive of some 230 yards that landed on the right edge of the fairway and rolled into the mustard.

Cloverjoy was now on the tee. He also had been advised by Barleycroft to aim his drive to the right. After several lusty practice swings, he blasted a long slice that traveled over the mustard and landed in a growth of peas along the fifteenth fairway. Barleycroft muttered something to Cloverjoy as they marched to the peas. After Cloverjoy's drive was found, Barleycroft launched a 3-wood from the rough back toward the fourteenth fairway.

The doctor's caddie, Bobby Clambourne, found Dick's drive at the edge of the mustard. The doctor dropped the ball in the short rough and hammered a 3-wood to just short of the green. At this point, I thought Dick and the doctor had a good chance of winning the hole. Cloverjoy was next to play, and he stroked a short-iron to about fifteen feet from the flagstick. Dick now had about a 10-yard pitch shot to the flag. He swung and appeared to hit just behind the ball, leaving a twenty-foot putt. Both pros missed the birdie putts, and the remaining putts were conceded. As they walked off the green, Dick muttered to me that they would have won the hole if he had hit a better approach shot.

The fifteenth hole was a par-3 of 185 yards. The doctor was on the tee, swinging easily with a 6-iron. I noted the hole was playing downwind. He then hit the 6-iron to the lower edge of the green, leaving Dick with a twenty-foot uphill putt. Barleycroft was now on the tee, and he smacked a 6-iron to the back edge of the green where it trickled over the side into a bunker. Cloverjoy entered the bunker, and after several practice swings, he blasted out over the green and into the bunker on the left. Barleycroft scowled as he took his stance in the bunker and blasted out to about five feet from the flag. Dick now had a ten-foot putt for birdie, or to par the hole, either of which would win the hole. He lined up the putt and rolled in a birdie. There was scattered applause from the spectators. He and the doctor were now 1-up.

The 400-yard sixteenth hole was halved with par, and it was on to the seventeenth, a 440-yard par-4 playing into the wind. Both pros drove into the spinach. Dick and Cloverjoy took a drop from the spinach into the rough that was three or four inches high. Cloverjoy was away, and he blasted out from the rough to the fairway, leaving a short-iron to the green. Dick did a little better, hammering an 8-iron farther down the fairway, leaving the doctor with a wedge shot to the green. Barleycroft then struck a 6-iron that landed on the green and spun back to no more than five feet from the cup. The doctor followed with a wedge shot that hit the pin and rolled about four feet from the cup.

Both writers now had par putts. Cloverjoy was away. He and Barleycroft lined up the putt, and then Cloverjoy hit a timid putt that stopped on the lip. Barleycroft wanted to wait several minutes to see if the putt would drop, but the doctor said he would give them one minute. Dick looked closely at the putt and said it was a quarter of an inch away and not on the edge of the hole. Consequently, Cloverjoy picked it up after the doctor conceded the remaining tap-in.

Dick had a chance to win the hole by sinking the four-footer. It appeared relatively straight, but when he stroked the putt, he appeared to have pulled it several inches offline. Both Dick and Cloverjoy appeared sick. The doctor walked over to Dick and reminded him they were still 1-up and to take several deep breaths before the upcoming tee shot on eighteen.

The eighteenth hole was a 565-yard par-5 dogleg to the right, playing downwind. For the first time in the match, all four players stood on the tee and surveyed the fairway. They all agreed the tomatoes, left of the fairway, offered the best target because the strip of rough surrounding the tomatoes wasn't too high, but this made the hole play a bit longer. Both Barleycroft and the doctor agreed the bunker where the fairway turned right wasn't too hazardous if a drive should roll into it. A player could escape from it with a 6-iron or even a 3-iron if the ball wasn't too near the edge.

Bobby Clambourne turned to Dick and said, "Hit it down the middle." Both pros chuckled over this advice.

Dick then took his stance, and after several practice swings, he belted a drive some 260 yards that drifted off the fairway and into the tomatoes.

Cloverjoy stood on the tee and I heard Barleycroft tell him to aim right and swing hard. If the drive cleared the bunker, it would shorten the hole and offer an opportunity for a birdie that might tie the match. I thought this idea was asking too much from his partner. With a determined look on his face, Cloverjoy took two quick practice swings and pulled a drive that hooked far to the left beyond the tomatoes. As the players walked down the fairway, the doctor remarked that he didn't know what the rough was like that far off the fairway. Clambourne admitted he hadn't scouted that far, but he guessed the rough was probably at least six inches high.

Barleycroft and Cloverjoy began thrashing through the rough and, surprisingly, found the errant drive in the deep rough. Barleycroft took several practice swings before blasting a shot enveloped in grass and turf. The shot barely made it to the fairway. Meanwhile, the doctor found Dick's drive among the tomatoes and dropped it in the short rough between the fairway and the tomatoes. He had a good lie and took his 3-wood and belted a shot that landed about fifty yards short of the green.

Cloverjoy had the next shot. He swung hard with a 3-wood and topped a shot that rolled some two hundred yards down the fairway. Barleycroft was next to hit; it was their fourth shot. He stroked a 6-iron to about twelve feet from the flag. The next shot was Dick's. He struck a wedge shot to about ten feet from the flag. Cloverjoy now had to sink his putt for par and hope his opponents would take three putts from ten feet. As he lined it up, Barleycroft walked off the green. Cloverjoy struck a good putt that barely missed on the right. This remaining putt was conceded. The doctor now had a ten-foot putt to end the match. He lined up the putt and rolled it in, winning the hole and the championship 2-up.

The gallery applauded loudly as Dick rushed over to the doctor and shook his hand. The doctor's wife broke from the gallery and gave her husband a big hug and a kiss. Likewise, Dick's wife rushed up to give him a hug. Cloverjoy walked over to Dick and the doctor and offered his congratulations. He then said that when he saw Dick's drive, he knew he had to hit at least as good a tee shot—or they would lose. I thought, *When Dick and the doctor saw Cloverjoy's drive land beyond the tomatoes, they must have sensed victory.*

I felt sorry for Cloverjoy. He didn't play badly, and the match did go eighteen holes. I didn't think Barleycroft offered him much support.

Dick was fortunate to have had Dr. Middlefield and his caddie as a partner. Barleycroft didn't play badly either. At times, his emotions seemed to affect his talent. Dick said he hoped Barleycroft would make an appearance at the clubhouse, although he might be too embarrassed about his walking off the green at the end of the match to appear.

On the clubhouse veranda, players from previous matches, their caddies, reporters, and guests were all enjoying champagne. Sir Harold was there to present a check to the winner, Dr. Middlefield, and the runner-up pro, Byford Barleycroft, who did make an appearance. A reporter asked the doctor what it was like to play with a sportswriter as a partner. The doctor answered that he enjoyed golf in its many presentations, and the Gnomewood tournament fit his expectations. He added, "Dick Whistle possesses a sound golf game, and I enjoyed playing with him." He turned to the group of sports reporters and said he expected his win would be properly reported in the sports sections of their respective publications. Barleycroft offered his congratulations to the doctor and Dick and said how much he enjoyed competing at Gnomewood. With that said, he and his brother waved goodbye and were off.

Sir Harold stepped forward and announced the clubhouse would close shortly, and only players, wives, and friends were invited to Excelsior House in about an hour. Dr. Middlefield thanked Sir Harold for his efforts in sponsoring the Gnomewood Seven-Club Challenge but said he and his wife had to leave so he could prepare for an upcoming tournament, the Sea Water Invitational, played on the Isle of Wight.

As the doctor and his wife left, I could see Edith Middlefield driving their Jaguar and the doctor sitting beside her, holding his clubs and a bottle of champagne.

Cloverjoy joined Dick, his wife, and me for the short ride to Excelsior House. Who should be standing at the entrance but Miss Forsythia Shotwell. She and Geoff exchanged a cautious handshake—along with offering her congratulations to Dick for being on the winning team. She had played several rounds with Dr. Middlefield in the past and had found him a delightful partner.

Sir Harold and his wife appeared and ushered us into a study for glasses of dry sherry. Also in the room were friends of Sir Harold's in the publishing business and a few members of the Sea Bird Society. Later in the evening, I found Sir Harold's interest in the yellow-breasted ratchet led to his becoming a member of the Sea Bird Society.

As we finished the sherry, Mrs. Gilroy announced dinner was ready. The first course was a lettuce and tomato salad picked fresh from the links. This was followed by a beef stew also containing locally grown vegetables. The meal was accompanied by champagne. I sat beside Benjamin Thistletoe, Fowler's brother, whom I discovered was a member of the Sea Bird Society. I asked about the Sea Bird Society, and he told me they studied various birds that roamed offshore, including gulls, fulmars, shearwaters, and petrels.

I mentioned the strange bird encountered on Gnomewood Links, the yellow-breasted ratchet, and he knew of the bird. He thought it was more of a shorebird than a seabird, but they sometimes feed many miles offshore, which, in the opinion of some ornithologists, qualifies them as seabirds. I asked if he had played golf at Gnomewood Links, and he replied, "Only rarely—and only when the various seabirds are in mating season. I study them in some detail. The ratchet is a very shy bird and is easily disturbed. Their disagreeable cry is a warning to those approaching their nests."

Thistletoe said he would suggest to Sir Harold that a sign be placed near their nesting area, warning those looking for lost balls that disturbing these birds would produce a most disagreeable noise.

During the dinner, Miss Shotwell was not sitting directly across from Cloverjoy, but she was near enough to engage in lively conversation.

When there was a lull in their conversation, I leaned over and asked Miss Shotwell if she had any plans to play in the States. She said she had considered trying to qualify for the US Women's Amateur but wasn't sure she wanted to compete in our USGA Women's Open. I said I thought she had a good chance of competing successfully but understood her reluctance to venture across the pond until she had more experience competing in Great Britain.

Dessert had been prepared by Soufflé and consisted of oranges, coconuts, and walnuts accompanied by a sauterne. I asked Cloverjoy if he would play in the Gnomewood tournament again. He replied that the experience would now play a role in how he reported a golf tournament in the future—and he would be honored to be invited back next year. I told him Sir Harold would be delighted to hear this.

I saw Dick and his wife rising from the table and wanted to get in a word of thanks for his influence in getting me the invitation to attend Gnomewood. After shaking hands, Dick told me to be alert for a letter from Sir Harold when I returned to the States. The letter would be more than a simple thank-you for attending the tournament, but he didn't elaborate further. Dick also said he would write to me about the V-1 explosion and the identity of the body when more information became available. I said I would look forward to that and waved goodbye to them as they boarded the bus to the train station.

The guests were starting to leave, and I said goodbye to Sir Harold and his wife. Sir Harold said he hoped to see me next year at Gnomewood, and I replied I would enjoy attending his tournament next year, providing my editor didn't have other assignments for me. He also requested I not report anything about the V-1 explosion when I return home. I said goodbye and boarded the bus to the Prince Rupert. I had packing to do and needed to jot down a few notes on the Gnomewood experience.

CHAPTER 8

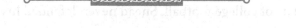

In the morning, I finished packing, briefly reviewed my notes about the Gnomewood tournament, and caught a train to London. I stayed overnight before flying back to New York.

My wife, Barbara, and daughter, Susan, were happy to see me and hear all about my trip to England. Barb, as she has in the past, helped me organize my notes into something comprehensible. I felt confident in submitting details of my trip to the senior editor, Eddie Malloy, and he trimmed it down so that it could be published in two parts in the Sunday edition. The response from the readers was positive, and Eddie expressed an interest in having me cover unique sporting events such as the Gnomewood Seven-Club Challenge.

In the meantime, I had local sports events to cover and plans to make to attend the Open to be played at Royal Lytham. However, at the last minute, Eddie canceled my trip to the Open, mainly because of a lack of interest in the British Open. No American had won there since Sam Snead back in 1946, and there didn't appear to be any serious contenders from the States making the trip to Scotland. He did hold out hope that I might cover the Ryder Cup, which was to be played in Scotland in October. In recent years, the Ryder Cup competition hadn't generated much interest because the American side had dominated competition. However, when I found out neither Snead nor Middlecoff were on the US team, my interest in covering this event waned. I decided not to attend.

In October, the American team lost the Ryder Cup despite winning the foursomes, taking three out of four matches. In the singles, Great Britain and Ireland prevailed. There was complaining by the Americans about the lodging, the food, and the weather. I'm glad I didn't witness the defeat.

I also didn't cover the Open. The lack of interest on the part of American professionals led to me staying in the States to cover baseball and the start of college football. Snead never defended his Open title in 1946. He claimed he lost money making the trip to St. Andrews. Hogan supposedly played in the Open in 1953 to add to his record of having won the four major tournaments: US Open, the Masters, the PGA, and the British Open. I thought it would take a rising, exciting young player such as Arnold Palmer to rekindle interest in the British Open in the States.

In October, I received a letter from Sir Harold. As I opened it, I wondered if he was thanking me for attending his tournament and writing a favorable account in the press or offering me a spot to play in his tournament. I had a slight feeling of apprehension as I unfolded the letter. There it was in writing: an invitation to attend next year's Seven-Club Challenge as a competitor. It took a minute for this to sink in before I read the rest of the letter. The letter stated the format would be a bit different next year in that there would be one day of stroke play to qualify before the sixteen teams of sportswriters and professionals were to be selected for match play. The qualifying would open the field to more players, but it would eliminate less skilled golfers. There would be an entrance fee of ten pounds. "Upon receiving an affirmative response, a room will be booked for you at the Prince Rupert." He added, "I look forward to seeing you next year at Gnomewood Links."

Of course, I accepted after obtaining approval from Barbara. I soon realized I would have to fit in golf practice this winter—along with my other assignments covering college football and ice hockey. As for practicing, one of my fellow sportswriters told me about an indoor golf practice facility at the YMCA. A young golf professional worked there in the winter, giving lessons to golfers of varying abilities.

During a lunch break, I walked over to the Y and spoke with the pro. He was glad to work with me in improving my shots. He recommended I bring my driver, 3-wood, and 5-iron for my first lesson. I scheduled lessons weekly for a month and then, pending improvement, saw him monthly until my trip to Gnomewood. This worked out well, and I achieved a proficiency greater than the modest skill I had initially demonstrated to him. He recommended that I add a 5-wood to my bag. This club was easier to hit than a long iron, and he recommended a Kenneth Burns model, which had a half-inch shorter shaft and a few degrees more loft than my 3-wood. I ordered it and looked forward to putting it in play when the golf season began in the spring.

CHAPTER 9

The first week in May, several of us sportswriters in the area organized a golf trip to upstate New York to play a course called Hope's Corner, near Poughkeepsie. The course was only 6,100 yards long and had few bunkers. I managed to break ninety the first day, but I was not at all satisfied with my score. I felt I needed to shoot in the low eighties on this course to make a decent showing at Gnomewood. The invitation from Sir Harold did not guarantee I would make the cut to qualify for match play.

After some practice at a nearby driving range, I managed to shoot an eighty-three the next day, but the others in the group also shot in the eighties. I realized this course was not very challenging, but I was pleased with my new 5-wood. I gained about ten yards distance compared to my 3-iron, and the higher loft of the 5-wood enabled me to hit and hold the green on two par-5 holes.

Over Memorial Day weekend, one of my senior editors invited me and two other sportswriters to play a round at National Golf Links, on Long Island, which tested the true state of my game. It was a sobering experience. I shot a ninety-eight. My driving was off, and my short game was not much better. I didn't putt too badly, but I realized I needed all the practice I could squeeze in before leaving for Gnomewood. My plan was to arrive at Gnomewood two days before the tournament began to sharpen my game.

In June, I covered the National Open at Southern Hills, which was won by Tommy Bolt. Upon returning home, I received a letter from Sir Harold reiterating the rules for the upcoming tournament at Gnomewood Links. There would be one day of qualifying, and the top sixteen golf writers and top professionals would be selected to play. The tournament committee, Sir Harold himself, would form the teams for the alternate shot play the next day. I was concerned I might not make the cut, but if not, I would be observing play and reporting it for readers back home.

As planned, I arrived at Gnomewood-by-Sea two days before the tournament started. A room had been reserved for me at the Prince Rupert. In the lobby of the Prince Rupert, there were two new carpets; otherwise, the interior looked much the same. At the reception desk, there was a note from Dick saying he would see me tomorrow at the practice range. After checking in, the clerk took my bag and golf clubs up to my room. I unpacked my bag, hung up my clothes, and unzipped the traveling bag containing my golf clubs. After inspecting my clubs for any sign of damage, I decided to head for the links. I wanted to get in some practice before dinner.

In the lobby, I recognized two golfers from last year: Fowler Thistletoe and Christopher Thinwood. We chatted briefly about the upcoming tournament and the need to practice. Both admitted they hadn't had much time to practice because of their respective reporting assignments.

They were eyeing my golf clubs, and Fowler asked if I might be playing in the tournament or had simply brought them along to practice and would be playing at Gnomewood after the tournament was completed.

I told them I had been invited to compete and might be the first American contestant. Neither could recall an American playing in Sir Harold's tournament. We talked briefly about the professionals who might be playing in this year's tournament. They knew Devereaux Dedmon had won a tournament in Croydon, and Colin Feathershanks had come in first at the Inverness Classic. We agreed they would be strong partners if one of us were paired with either of them.

Christopher asked if I had been guaranteed a spot in the tournament or, if I failed to qualify, would I then return to the States or stay to report on the tournament. I said I was planning on reporting the tournament regardless of whether I was competing or not. We then agreed we should take a cab to Gnomewood Links and start practicing since the shuttle bus wasn't running yet.

The cab dropped us off at the clubhouse, and Leffingwell and Grafton greeted us with vigorous handshakes. Grafton took my clubs and said there were practice balls on the range. If we wished, we should feel free to start practicing. Thistletoe and Thinwood started to practice and I joined them on the range and started to hit wedge shots. Behind the three of us, I heard a voice who asked what amateurs were doing on the practice range. We looked around and saw the red slacks of Byford Barleycroft. He started to laugh and said we looked like we needed all the practice we could get. He asked me what I was doing practicing before the tournament.

I told him I was playing this year, provided I qualified, and he turned to Fowler and Christopher and said he hoped one of them would be worthy of being my partner. He then started to practice.

I practiced for about two hours and was reasonably pleased with how I was hitting my shots. I watched the two writers and Barleycroft hitting and thought they were in good form. Returning to the clubhouse, I stowed my clubs in a locker. Grafton was in the clubhouse, and I asked if he was heading back to the hotel soon. He said he would be glad to drive me to the Prince Rupert, and I accepted his offer.

Back at the Prince Rupert, I headed for the bar, which was now named the Bear & Owl. Livingston Phogg-Smythe and Bob Paltry were inside. I greeted Phogg-Smythe, commenting I hardly recognized him without his purple attire. Likewise, I commented on Paltry not wearing the lemon-yellow clothing he wore last year. He laughed and said he might wear a different color this year, but he didn't say what it was. Both expressed surprise that I was here this year. Paltry said my editor must have liked what I wrote about Gnomewood last year.

I didn't mention I was playing in the tournament this year. They would find out soon enough.

Paltry said he had been taking a few lessons to cure his tendency to slice, but if he was playing with friends for a modest wager, the slice creeps back at the worst time. Phogg-Smythe said he has been practicing his putting. A book on putting, *A Stroke of Confidence*, by Hamilton Smart, had been helpful. He hoped to see Smart in this year's tournament and relate to him the benefits of his book. As to with whom Paltry and Phogg-Smythe might be paired, Paltry had read that Devereaux Dedmon had won a recent tournament and would make a good partner. Phogg-Smythe agreed and added that the doctor was reported to be playing well and could lead his partner into the winner's circle. After a quick beer, I excused myself and headed for supper and then to bed.

In the morning, I returned to the practice range. The pros Byf Barleycroft, Giles Nippengay, and Harry Vardon Taylor were already on the range. When Nippengay saw my clubs, he asked if I was playing this year or just practicing.

Barleycroft answered, "Of course he is playing."

I said, "Byf saw me hit a few wedge shots yesterday and was impressed with my form."

The other two pros invited me to play a round with them as soon as they had warmed up. After about fifteen minutes, they said we should practice putting before teeing off. I agreed, and we headed for the practice green. Andy Quickfoot and Mel Camberwick were just finishing practice, and they asked if we wanted to join them as a fivesome. We agreed since it was only a practice round—and no one else was on the course.

Our tee shots all missed the fairway. I was the shortest, off the fairway, to the right. Barleycroft was the longest, but he hooked his tee shot into the left rough. The other two drives were about twenty yards beyond me, in the artichokes. I used my 5-wood for my second shot, the ball landing on the green and running off the back. The pros all hit the green with their second shots and two-putted for par. I hit a poor chip onto the green and had to settle for bogie.

On the second hole, the pros hit drivers and short irons to the green. I noted that they were playing with more than seven clubs in their golf bags and assumed they were testing which seven clubs they would use in the tournament. They all had a driver, a 3-wood, and a full set of irons and a putter. Barleycroft also had a 2-wood.

The pros shot par on the second hole. I bogied it, and it was on to the third hole. There, I scrambled for par. We all shot par until the sixth hole. There, we all aimed right toward the carrot patch. I faded a drive that landed in the rough just short of the carrots. Nippengay drove to the right edge of the fairway, while Barleycroft and Taylor both landed in the carrots.

I saw the stakes painted green and white, marking the drop zone, which Sir Harold had instituted this year. This avoided the deliberation in previous years over where to drop the ball that had landed in the vegetables. Previously, players had sometimes argued that a ball had been dropped too close to the green or that a ball was dropped in an area where the rough was shorter. Both pros hit the green with their shots from the drop zone and two-putted for par. From the fairway, Nippengay struck a short-iron to about three feet from the flagstick and holed the putt for a birdie. I managed to par the hole by sinking a twenty-foot putt. I bogied the next three holes for a forty-four on the front nine.

I wasn't much better on the back nine, coming in with another forty-four, giving me a total of eighty-eight. The pros were all at or near par and were sure to make the cut. As I walked off the green, I said I wasn't sure I would make the cut and qualify to play in the tournament. The pros, based on previous years' play, assured me I would have no trouble qualifying. Barleycroft added that I would probably be among the leading "sports liars."

I should have returned to the practice range, but I was too tired after the round with the pros. They said they were returning to the putting green, complaining about birdie putts they missed.

I headed to the clubhouse and saw Mel Camberwick and Andy Quickfoot. I asked Mel what he shot, and he said he didn't keep score, but he had played several shots on certain holes to see which club worked best. He thought Andy shot a seventy-five or seventy-six. I mentioned I shot an eighty-eight, and Mel thought that would qualify, probably in the middle of the field of golf writers. I replied that I needed to concentrate on my good shots, especially with my 5-wood, and, with a little more practice, I thought I could shoot in the low eighties. He asked if he could swing my 5-wood, and I pulled it from my bag and let him swing it a few times. He asked about the swing weight, and I said it was a D-3. "That's about right," he said. "Good luck tomorrow."

In the clubhouse, several new arrivals were planning to visit the practice range. They asked if I had been on the course, and I told them I had just finished playing and had observed the green-and-white stakes marking the drop zone by the vegetables. This was something new, and they assumed Sir Harold would explain this new rule before the qualifying started tomorrow.

The two Scotsmen arrived, Ian Crankshaw and Colin Feathershanks, and I suggested we take a beer and go out on the veranda. They both commented on how green the links appeared. Where they came from, there had been a dry spell, and the fairways had a brownish color in certain areas, but they added the ground was quite firm and their drives rolled another ten or twenty yards farther.

We glanced at the practice range and saw a lithesome figure hitting drives some 230–240 yards. It had to be Miss Shotwell. A younger girl was tossing balls to her to tee up. We watched her for a few minutes, and Ian commented about how easy she made hitting a golf ball appear. We agreed she made driving the ball appear smooth and trouble-free. I asked the others who were also watching if she might be playing in the tournament or perhaps practicing for a future event. Maynard Cumbersome gave me a quizzical look and said we would find out soon enough.

After she finished practice, I waited several minutes before approaching her and introduced myself as the sportswriter from the States who had attended last year's Gnomewood tournament. I said, "Several sportswriters were watching you hit drives and admired your swing."

She smiled and said she appreciated their appraisal of her swing—and she hoped she would play well in this year's tournament.

I was quite surprised to hear this, and after several seconds, I responded, "So you are playing in Sir Harold's tournament?"

She answered "Yes, and you are the Yank who might be my partner."

I suppose I looked stunned, but I recovered quickly enough to say it would be a privilege to her partner.

She said, "I hope to be on the winning team."

I felt shaky. I could only say I had been practicing over the winter but had only played a few times this spring. Fortunately, she didn't ask about my handicap or my recent scores.

One of the writers standing next to me muttered, "Lucky you."

Miss Shotwell introduced me to the young lady carrying her golf bag as her younger sister Rose. "We call her Rosie, and please call me Sissy."

I told her to call me John because Mr. Nelson was too formal. I said I would see her at the start of qualifying.

They turned and walked to the putting green, and she said, "See you tomorrow."

I returned to the practice range and spent nearly an hour, hoping to gain a few yards of distance. I didn't see any definite improvement.

Toward the other end of the range, Dick Whistle was practicing with a noisy group of players whom I judged to be sports reporters in their late twenties. I waved to Dick, and he waved back and walked over to greet me. He commented on my participating at Gnomewood and was sure I would have an experience worth writing about.

I said, "I met Miss Shotwell, and she seems confident that I could be her partner."

Dick nodded and said, "You are now the favorite." He smiled and added, "If you qualify."

I said, "I realize that and hope to at least make a good showing."

Dick said he needed to practice to make sure he qualified, and he returned to the group of noisy young men at the end of the range.

CHAPTER 10

In the clubhouse, a group of sportswriters was enjoying a beverage. The talk was about who among the professionals was "on their game" and who would be a desirable partner. Dick said he had recently attended the Northern Scottish Masters, a unique tournament played for the first two days at Nairn and the last two days at Royal Dornoch. Colin Feathershanks was the winner, shooting a sixty-six in the final round. Pylton Suggs and Tommy Sapwood finished in the top ten.

I asked how Miss Shotwell was progressing in amateur competition, and Dick said she had been successful and was planning to remain an amateur. Thus far, her father has been able to support her practice and travel to tournaments, and she didn't want to travel to the States to try the professional circuit. I thought this was a wise decision, and I reminded those listening that if she competed in the States, she would face stiff competition from American players such as Patty Berg, Louise Suggs, Betsy Rawls, and a new addition to the professional ranks, Mickey Wright. Miss Shotwell had expressed an interest in entering the US Women's Amateur next year, depending on how well she was playing this season. Her play in this year's Gnomewood tournament would help determine her future tournament schedule. Upon hearing this, I became more apprehensive about competing as her partner. I didn't want the possibility of my poor play to influence her performance in the upcoming tournament.

A noisy group of young men with golf bags headed for the practice range. I assumed a train from London had arrived and suspected they had stopped at the Rake & Dibble before heading for Gnomewood Links.

Phogg-Smythe expressed his doubt about their qualifications to play in the tournament, but he assumed Sir Harold had invited them to play. Their presence might liven up the tournament and enhance their careers as sports reporters. Christopher Thinwood, Phogg-Smythe, and I decided to follow this vociferous group to the practice range and observe their behavior.

Several professionals on the range stopped practicing when the young reporters began scrambling for practice balls. Thinwood thought he recognized a few of them, but he couldn't recall where they were employed. He walked over to one of the young men and introduced himself. The young man was Reginald Grayfield, a reporter for the *Salisbury Standard*. I overheard Grayfield say he was new to the game and, as a new sportswriter, he wanted to learn more about the game. I noted a mixed assortment of clubs in his bag, one of which had a wooden shaft. I thought his chances for qualifying were nil, but he would gain some experience in tournament golf.

Dick and the Shotwell girls walked from the clubhouse back to the range. They had heard the noisy group of new arrivals and were curious about their identities. We watched several of them practice, and I quickly determined who had some experience playing golf and who was struggling to just hit the ball.

Dick said he recognized one who was struggling to just hit the ball as Reginald Cockling, a young reporter for the *Sheffield Sports Beacon*. Dick introduced himself, and during their conversation, I learned that Reginald had been reporting on football and was hoping for some golf assignments. I excused myself from the group and departed for the clubhouse. I didn't want to watch him flailing at the ball.

Walking back to the clubhouse, I saw a young man approaching, whom I assumed was another reporter. He was carrying a large brown leather golf bag with a motley assortment of clubs. I stopped and introduced myself. He said his name was Bradley Brackenfield, and he was hoping to qualify for Sir Harold's tournament. I commented on the number of clubs in his bag and said I hoped he would be able to decide as he practiced which seven clubs he would use in the tournament.

He answered that he thought you were supposed to have at least seven clubs in your bag. He had obtained the bag and clubs from his uncle, who had qualified for the Open in 1935.

I explained that the rules in Sir Harold's tournament limited a player to just seven clubs.

He muttered something about where he could store the extra clubs, and I told him I was sure someone in the clubhouse would help him. "Good luck," I said as I continued my walk back to the clubhouse. When he reached the practice range, he would probably find help in sorting out which clubs to use.

In the clubhouse, a short, ruddy-faced, partially bald man was regaling those enjoying their beers with his accounts of attempting to swim the English Channel. He was confident that a story about the attempt written by a participant would hold a reader's attention. John Rogie, a sportswriter for the *Dover Globe*, had acquired the nickname of "Splash Rogie." His previous attempts to swim the channel had failed. First, he claimed he got lost in a school of mackerel and had to be rescued. Another attempt was aborted when he claimed he was attacked by a giant squid. The attacker proved to be a remnant of a fishing net. Other attempts failed because of high seas, but he said he was planning another attempt as soon as he found a sponsor.

I was standing near Bob Paltry, and I asked if he knew if Rogie was planning to play in Sir Harold's tournament.

"I'm afraid so," Bob replied. "Sir Harold had no idea what Rogie's handicap was, but he thought inviting Rogie to play would attract more spectators and make a good story in the newspapers."

Dick had returned from the practice range, and after hearing about

Rogie's attempt at qualifying, he said, "I hope he has better luck playing golf than in swimming the channel."

We decided it was time for dinner and took the bus to the Prince Rupert.

At dinner, I brought up the issue of bad golfers and what pro would want to play with them—should they be lucky enough to qualify. Dick said he had heard a rumor that Sir Harold had invited several sportswriters who had handicaps of at least twenty—or maybe they thought a handicap was a bad slice.

We all agreed Sir Harold must have considered this issue and would have a solution. Later, Leffingwell announced that Sir Harold would be arriving at the clubhouse with the schedule for qualifying starting at eight—and play would start at nine. There was some grumbling about the fact that a player might not have a starting time until later in the morning and would have to sit around the clubhouse before starting to warm up—and the fact that the field might be clogged with golf misfits. Those who had played previously at Gnomewood advised simply waiting and seeing what tomorrow brings.

I was tired of hearing complaining, and after dinner and wine had induced a pleasant fatigue, I excused myself and retired to my room.

CHAPTER 11

The alarm awakened me from a sound sleep. I shaved, dressed quickly, and headed for the dining room. A notice posted at the dining room entrance informed the golfers that the qualifying times would now be posted at nine o'clock, and the first group would tee off at ten. This should allow adequate practice time for those teeing off at ten.

I sat down at the table with Maynard Cumbersome, Derick Marblehead, and Charleton Hicks-Joly. They were pleased that the starting time had been pushed back an hour. Hicks-Joly said he would not be playing this year, but he would be reporting the event for the *Buckinghamshire Sports Weekly*. His game was not in good form, and he didn't want to drag down his pro partner as he feels he did last year. His partner was Reggie Turnbuckle. Maynard reminded Hicks-Joly that they lost to the defending champions, which was nothing to be ashamed of. We finished breakfast, enjoyed a cigarette, and left the dining room to wait outside for the bus to Gnomewood Links.

Arriving at the clubhouse, I estimated about half the competitors had started to practice even though the playing times had not yet been posted. Dick was among those practicing. I asked him why the early practice. He suspected he would be among those starting at ten or shortly thereafter. I was puzzled by his answer, but I didn't want to further interrupt his practice by explaining to me why he felt he would be teeing off among the early groups attempting to qualify. I watched the players, both pros and sportswriters, hitting balls for a few minutes before returning to the clubhouse to wait for Sir Harold to post the pairings and starting times.

Shortly before nine, Sir Harold drove up to the clubhouse in his new motorized golf cart. In his hand were several sheets listing the starting times for the qualifying round. Golfers on the practice range grabbed their clubs and rushed to the clubhouse. I found my starting time was ten thirty, and I was playing with Dick and a professional, David Knibbles, who was new to the Gnomewood tournament. Dick had returned from the practice range, and I asked him about Knibbles. He said he was a steady player who made few mistakes. He would be an asset to the Gnomewood tournament. I noted that Dr. Middlefield, Forsythia Shotwell, and Giles Nippengay were at the twelve o'clock time. Miss Shotwell *was* playing in the tournament. I counted a total of forty-five golfers attempting to qualify. With a starting field of thirty-two, thirteen would not make the match play.

I saw the sportswriter Arthur Mountbank, whom I had met last year, jotting down several names, and I asked him who he was going to follow tomorrow. He greeted me and said the noon group had gotten his attention. He wondered how the young lady amateur would hold up playing with two excellent professionals. He then asked how an American had gotten into the tournament. I told him my handicap of twelve was just right. He laughed, said, "Good luck," and approached several other golfers in the clubhouse.

I was interested in the leadoff group, none of whom I recognized from last year's tournament. They were the pro Winston Peebles and two writers, Christian Hazeltree and Reginald Grayfield. I had met Grayfield yesterday on the practice range and had learned he was a newcomer to the game. He could easily slow down the starting group, but Sir Harold must have had a reason for putting him in the first group. The next group included "Phloosie" Archibald, Patrick Quigly, and Cliff Halestork. Archibald has been a frequent visitor to Gnomewood at tournament time, hoping to be chosen to play if a sportswriter had to drop out. Dick had said Phloosie was probably an eighteen handicap or higher. Again, I was concerned that Archibald's slow play would lead to frequent delays and result in a five-hour round of golf.

Someone called to my attention and to those around me that Sir Harold had posted a second sheet in the clubhouse. This sheet contained two important statements. First, any player with a score of fifty-five or higher at the end of the first nine holes would be withdrawn from competition. Second, a green-and-white stake would be placed outside of the vegetable-growing areas. A ball landing in the vegetables was to be retrieved and dropped within two club lengths from the stake, no nearer the hole. The stakes on each hole would be moved to a different location each day of the tournament. I decided this rule was put in place to avoid players dropping nearer the hole from the vegetables or playing to one side to avoid a bunker near the hole. This should eliminate any controversy as to where a drop should be made and speed up play.

I decided to watch the first group tee off to give me an indication as to the pace of play. Since the regular announcer, Harley Bellows, was absent because of another commitment, Sir Harold announced each contestant on the first tee. First off was Reginald Grayfield. He hit a weak drive that wiggled down the fairway about 150 yards. Hazeltree, the sportswriter, was next. He smacked a long slice that disappeared into the artichokes. The pro Peebles stepped to the tee, and after two quick practice swings, he belted a drive some 240 yards down the middle.

I followed this group to see how Hazeltree would play his second shot. After searching in the artichokes for about a minute, he retrieved his ball and moved to the green-and-white stake. He hesitated for a few seconds before Peebles walked over to the green and white stake, pulled Hazeltree's driver from his bag, and placed it on the ground two club lengths from the stake. The driver was picked up after a tee had been inserted in the ground to mark the extent of the drop area and Hazeltree dropped the ball over his shoulder into the drop area. He took two practice swings and hit an iron shot that bounced onto the green. Meanwhile, Grayfield's shot from the fairway rolled just short of the green. Peebles then struck an iron that landed on the right side of the green, about twelve feet from the flagstick. The three golfers proceeded to the green, and I thought, with Peebles's help, they would maintain a reasonable pace of play. It was time for me to start warming up.

I practiced for about an hour and then took a cigarette break. From the edge of the practice range, I could see the sixth hole. The starting threesome was approaching the hole. I decided to walk over to the green and follow play. I saw a player hit his drive about 250 yards to the right and into the carrots. I suspected it was Peebles. The next player hit a tee shot that landed at the beginning of the carrot patch, at least two hundred yards short of the green. The last player in the group hit what started as a good drive, but at the last second, it hooked into the elephant grass. I hoped he would hit a provisional ball since there was a chance the ball would be lost, but he didn't. I watched them walk to their respective drives.

Peebles accompanied the player who had hit his drive into the high grass, and they spent several minutes searching for the ball before Hazeltree looked back at the sixth tee. If his ball was lost, he would have to go back to the tee and hit again. Peebles grabbed his arm and led him to a site where Peebles had laid a club outside the high grass and instructed Hazeltree to drop a ball there. I thought they were declaring an unplayable lie without finding the ball. At least this would not delay the play too much.

It was getting near our starting time, and I walked to the practice putting green. Dick and the pro, David Knibbles, who would be playing with us, were practicing. Dick introduced me to Knibbles, a muscular young man who I judged to be about thirty years old. I told Knibbles I hoped some of his game would rub off on me. He smiled and said he would help me qualify if I asked for help. However, he added that he wasn't going to act as instructor during the round. Dick mentioned that he had been talking with Grafton earlier, and the schedule was running at least twenty minutes behind. Dick and I decided to return to the clubhouse for a cup of tea. Knibbles said he was going to practice putting a bit longer and would join us at the first tee.

In the clubhouse, we obtained our tea and sat down at a table with Geoff Cloverjoy, a young sportswriter. Geoff and I lit a cigarette, and Dick fiddled with his pipe. After lighting it, Dick asked what we knew about the body found during last year's tournament. I said I knew nothing about the final report, and Geoff said he had heard the investigation had been ongoing, but he was not aware of any final report.

Dick relit his pipe and filled us in on what had transpired after the body had been found when the V-1 blew up during the rainstorm. The body had been a member of the East German embassy. MI-5 concluded he had been instructed to procure the V-1—or at least obtain the engine and any part of the fuel system. The East Germans had planned to construct their own missile and not rely on the Soviets, who might not want one of their satellites making weapons for their own use. The V-1, or parts of it, were to be placed on a leased truck and taken to a site where the parts would be smuggled out of the country. The body was traced to the East Germans through the leased truck. Probably others who were involved had escaped. The East German embassy never officially identified the body, but some months later, they reported a member of their staff as having defected. Probably because of the time that had elapsed between when the V-1 had landed in 1945 and when the attempt was made to obtain all or parts of it, the East Germans assumed the bomb was inactive, but they were obviously wrong. The storm served as a cover for the attempt, and the force of the wind undoubtedly pushed the nose farther into the sand and detonated it. The other possibility was that the efforts to obtain the engine and guidance system were enough to cause the explosion.

Dick paused to relight his pipe. He then asked if Geoff and I had known about the relationship between Dedmon and Soufflé. I said I had overheard them speaking French, but I thought they were discussing French cuisine. In fact, Soufflé was his code name as an undercover agent in the war. He had been responsible for obtaining German plans for defending the Normandy coast against the Allied invasion. Dedmon, who had been a pickpocket before the war, had been instrumental in stealing plans from drunken German soldiers and passing them on to Soufflé's resistance group.

Just before the invasion, Soufflé and Dedmon were smuggled out of France to avoid being caught by the Gestapo. Soufflé had been trained as a chef and remained in England after the war. He had been employed by several restaurants in London and several seaside resorts along the English coast. Sir Harold had met him in London several years ago and persuaded him to work at his London home and at Gnomewood.

After hearing this story, I said someone should interview them about their wartime activities, but Dick said the two were reluctant to talk about their wartime experiences. I glanced at my watch and said we should resume warming up. Geoff agreed and immediately left the table to start practice.

Dick and I gazed at the practice range before we started to warm up. There was a familiar figure on the range. It was Si Bumly. He was wearing the same fishing hat he wore last year and was exhibiting the same lunging swing that was so repeatable that it made you wonder if other hackers might benefit from trying to duplicate it. Byford Barleycroft was easily identified by his red golf slacks. Dick noted that Barleycroft was shaking his head as he stared at Bumbry's swing. Were the two of them part of the 11:20 or 11:30 starting time? We both thought Barleycroft would not be pleased playing alongside Bumbrey. Bad shots were contagious.

Meanwhile, Grafton had walked back through the front nine to observe how qualifying was progressing. Upon his return, he was not encouraging us to start practice. Several groups were playing slowly, and he estimated it would take the first group at least another half an hour to finish the front nine. Dick suggested to Grafton that he speak to Sir Harold at the first tee as he introduced the players and cautioned them about slow play.

Within a few minutes, we heard the motorcycle roar. Grafton was in the driver's seat, and Sir Harold was in the sidecar. They headed for the ninth tee, and Sir Harold began ushering the players past the refreshment cart and on to the tenth tee. Dick assured Sir Harold we would start practicing if play was sped up. If there were further delays, we could spend more time on the putting green.

On the practice range, the pros Reggie Turnbuckle, Pylton Suggs, and Tommy Sapwood were warming up. Alongside them were the sportswriters Geoff Cloverjoy, Phil Frogwell-Potts, and Patrick Quigley, a rosy-faced Irishman. Quigley expressed his delight in being invited to the Gnomewood tournament. He was intrigued by the name Gnomewood, and Dick referred him to a pamphlet in the clubhouse that would provide a history of the links. I told him an old gentleman in the clubhouse would gladly tell him the history of the vegetables grown on the links. Quigley asked if a score in the midnineties would qualify for match play. Dick was diplomatic and said it probably would, but if the wind increased, qualifying scores were difficult to predict. Quigley thanked us for the advice and adjourned to the clubhouse bar. Other golfers were resorting to spirits to put a sharp edge to their play before teeing off.

As we started to practice, I asked Dick to hit a few shots with my new 5-wood, and he was impressed. He remarked that he had an old Dunlap 4-wood that didn't compare with my 5-wood in distance and accuracy. For most amateurs, he thought the 5-wood was more effective than the 3-iron. We practiced for about twenty minutes before we observed several players on the practice putting green. This indicated the schedule was still behind. I suggested we return to the clubhouse for a quick snack.

Inside the clubhouse, we met Miss Shotwell and her younger sister, Rose. Miss Shotwell recognized me as "Mr. Nelson, the Yank who had come over to try his luck at winning Sir Harold's tournament." I responded that I hoped to make a credible showing in competing against what I knew would be a strong field. I asked Rose if she would be a caddie for her sister, and she said yes. She hoped to gain some experience as a caddie for her sister in tournament play.

Our snack consisted of hot buttered toast and sliced apples, and Soufflé brought fish and chips for the Shotwell girls. As we finished, Dick said good luck to the Shotwell girls.

Miss Shotwell replied, "Maybe we will meet in a match during the tournament."

I thought, *Maybe if I qualify.*

Since the putting green was empty, Dick and I decided on some last-minute practice. We both wondered where the pro Winston Peebles was, the third member of our group. Just then, from the clubhouse, emerged a figure in dark slacks and a white shirt with an open collar. He walked up to us and introduced himself as Oliver Marsden, a sportswriter from Swindon. He informed us that Mr. Peebles had joined an earlier group that looked as though they needed professional help. Oliver was of a portly build, wore thick glasses, and had a ruddy face, indicating he had spent some time outdoors. He said he had covered horse racing in the past, but he found reporting golf more creative. He expanded further, stating golf took three to four hours to cover, while a horse race was over in just a few minutes, meaning you had to rush your appraisal of what you had witnessed to your newspaper. Furthermore, the horse must speak through the jockey, who may or may not be very articulate. In golf, with the proper questions, the player will expand on the round just completed and even embellish certain shots that you may not have observed as being that well played.

CHAPTER 12

Oliver was using an old Cruickshank putter with a wooden shaft and was rolling putts at the hole with some expertise. I felt confident he would not have too many three-putt greens that would delay play. We heard the names of the players preceding us on the first tee, picked up our golf bags, and waited behind the tee. Harry Vardon Taylor was on the tee and led off with a drive some 240 yards down the middle. Two sportswriters followed him and hit meandering drives short of the artichokes.

Our names were now called, and we scampered up the teeing area to acknowledge the scant applause from the small gallery. Dick led off and smacked a long fade of about 240 yards that just missed the artichokes. Oliver was next up. He pulled a battered driver from his bag, and after a quick practice swing, he hit a drive about 230 yards down the middle. I was up. After a nervous practice swing, I smacked a drive about 230 yards that drifted to the left edge of the fairway. I breathed a sigh of relief as we marched down the fairway to our respective drives.

We managed to par the first three holes. Oliver got his par on the third hole by sinking a twenty-foot putt. Dick and I looked at each other and nodded in agreement. *This man can play.*

The fifth hole was our undoing. At 390 yards, it should have been a possible birdie hole, but poor bunker play by Oliver and me and Dick's hitting over the green, plus weak chip shots and three-putting resulted in double bogies for the three of us. We all scored bogies on the sixth hole. Oliver drove into the elephant grass and was lucky to escape with a bogie. Dick and I drove into the carrots, and, after taking a drop, faded our second shots into one of the pot bunkers to the right of the green. We played decent bunker shots to the flagstick, but we missed par putts. We recovered our form on the seventh and eighth holes and scored par. On the ninth hole, a long par-5, we all settled for par. Oliver sank a thirty-foot putt for his par. At the end of nine, we were all three over par.

Starting the back nine, we all felt confident we would quality for match play tomorrow if we could maintain our current level of play. Dick and I parred the tenth hole. The 212-yard eleventh hole was into wind, and I used my 3-iron but was short of the green. I should have used my 5-wood. I chipped to about five feet from the cup but missed my par putt. Dick also missed a relatively short putt for bogie. Oliver missed the green on his tee shot, and the ball landed in the lettuce. He then chipped twenty feet past the flagstick and missed his par putt for a bogie. We all parred the relatively short twelfth hole. Dick and Oliver parred the 145-yard thirteenth, and I was in the small bunker on the right and failed to get down in two for a bogie.

The fourteenth hole, a par-5, played into the wind. Dick and I were fortunate to par it. My 5-wood helped me hit the green on my third shot. Oliver took a bogie. On the fifteenth hole, a par-3 playing downwind, Dick and I overshot the green. Oliver noted our tee shots and underclubbed, hitting his tee shot into the peas. Poor chip shots led to bogies. At that point, I was plus 6, Dick was plus 5, and Oliver was plus 7.

The sixteenth hole, a par-4, played downwind, and we all hit drives in the 230–240 range. Crisp iron shots left Dick and me with birdie putts in the ten-foot range that we failed to sink but made an easy par. Oliver had at least a forty-foot putt that he almost sank, leaving him a tap-in for par.

The 440-yard seventeenth played into the wind, and none of us reached the green in two strokes. Our approach shots were also short, and mine landed in the spinach. We managed to hit the green with our third shot, but we were left with putts of twelve-to-fifteen feet. Our par putts were also short.

The eighteenth hole was a 565-yard dogleg right. I hit my best drive, a 260-yard blast that left me with a 5-wood to the green. Dick attempted to cut the dogleg, but his drive landed in a fairway bunker. Oliver hooked his drive into the tomato patch. From there, his 3-wood landed in the fairway—but well short of the green. Dick had to use a short-iron from the bunker and then a 6-iron to reach the green. Oliver hit a 3-iron to the edge of the green. My 5-wood left me an 8-iron to the green, which I stroked to about six feet from the flagstick. Dick and I two-putted for par. Oliver took three putts for a bogie.

At the end of eighteen holes, Dick was plus 6, I was plus 7, and Oliver was plus 9. I was thrilled to have broken eighty for the first time in several years. Oliver was concerned that he might not qualify for match play, but Dick assured him he would have no problem, given the quality of play by some of the sportswriters in the field.

Back in the clubhouse, we posted our scores. From earlier rounds, we saw Colin Feathershanks had shot seventy-three, and Pylton Suggs and David Knibbles had shot seventy-four. The three of us decided to take a beer out on the veranda and watch the players finish.

After several minutes, I saw Miss Shotwell on the sixteenth green. Miss Shotwell, Dr. Middlefield, and Giles Nippengay were lining up putts, probably birdie putts on this par-4 hole. Each missed their putts, but all three sank the remaining tap-ins.

The three moved on to the seventeenth tee. Miss Shotwell had the honors. She blasted a long drive into the wind that hooked into the spinach. Nippengay and the doctor hit drives that were down the middle, and the doctor's was longer. Nippengay struck a wood that reached the base of the green. Miss Shotwell was next to play. She removed her ball from the spinach and dropped it by the green-and-white stake. After taking several practice swings with what appeared to be a long iron, she stroked a shot of some two hundred yards to the left side of the green. The doctor then played what appeared to be a midiron to the green. The three all appeared to par the hole, moved to the eighteenth tee, and had to wait.

Bumly, Barleycroft, and Marblehead were still on the eighteenth fairway. Bumly was the first to hit. With his characteristic lunge, he swung and topped the ball that ran to the edge of the tomatoes. The other two players then hit 3-woods from where their drives had landed that, with the aid of the wind, landed and rolled to near the edge of the green. Bumly then thumped an iron that made it to the fairway about 150 yards from the green. He then topped another shot that rolled onto the green about forty feet from the flagstick. Eventually, the three players putted out. It struck me that Barleycroft never appeared to watch Bumly strike the ball on the fairway or on the green.

Shotwell, Nippengay, and the doctor all hit long drives and followed with fairway woods that landed fifty-to-sixty yards short of the green. Their approach shots landed in birdie range, but only the doctor appeared to sink his putt for a birdie.

After finishing on eighteen, Leffingwell drove Miss Shotwell to Excelsior House.

The doctor and Nippengay waved to us as they entered the clubhouse.

CHAPTER 13

Inside the clubhouse, smoke and the smell of spilled beer permeated the air, and a howling horde of golfers recounted their play. There was a slight pause in the noise as Dr. Middlefield's score of sixty-eight was posted—along with Miss Shotwell's score of seventy-four. Dick said there was some betting that she wouldn't break eighty. Several players congratulated the doctor on his score. He thanked them and pointed out the favorable playing conditions: "The course was there for the taking. Tomorrow could be quite different in regard to wind, different drop locations, different hole locations on the greens, and the tees being moved back."

Since Byf Barleycroft had qualified with a seventy-seven, Bumly's play didn't adversely affect Barleycroft's score. Dick led the sportswriters with his seventy-eight, and my seventy-nine brought slight applause and a "Good show, Yank." Oliver was delighted he had qualified. Several sportswriters failed to qualify, including Brad Bramblefield, "Splash" Rogie, Uncliffe Sixbee, Reggie Grayfield, and several others who were escorted off the links without completing eighteen holes.

I overheard two pros who had failed to qualify complaining about the sportswriters in their respective threesomes. They claimed neither writer would have broken one hundred if they hadn't been removed from the qualifying round. Their inept play was a constant distraction, and neither pro regained their form during the remaining holes. Sir Harold had instituted the qualifying round to eliminate certain sportswriters who had been pestering him to play at Gnomewood. A pro who happened to be playing with a bumbling writer should have somehow guarded against this situation.

The bus pulling up to the clubhouse was a welcome sound. I needed to get back to the Prince Rupert to jot down some notes on today's play. On the bus, several disgruntled sportswriters complained about the pros in their groups. Foster Ravenswood said, "He kept giving advice about the grain of the grass when I putted, and I couldn't see it. This completely confused me." Fortunately, the ride was short, and I didn't have to listen to the various excuses about poor play for very long.

At the Prince Rupert, I went to my room for a shower and a quick nap. Dick had said he would meet me in the dining room later after he had written his notes on the day's play. I wanted a quick nap and set my alarm for an hour; I didn't want to sleep through dinnertime.

An hour later, I awakened by the alarm, put on a clean shirt, and strolled down to the dining room, which was now named the Bunch of Carrots. The bar across the hall, which previously had been the Bunch of Carrots, was now called the Bear & Owl. Sir Harold had purchased two wooden carvings of a bear and an owl, standing about three feet tall, and placed them at the entrance to the bar. I thought these figures added more of a pub-like atmosphere to the bar. In the bar, a few golfers were imbibing in their favorite spirits.

In the dining room, I found an empty chair at a table occupied by Geoff Cloverjoy and a character named "Phoosie" Archibald. Archibald was a stout, red-faced fellow whom I had met last year, hanging around the clubhouse. He had played in the Gnomewood tournament several years ago, and according to Dick, he was not regarded by the pros as someone whom you would like as a partner. He said he was a semiretired sportswriter who wrote occasional articles for the *Atlantic Golfer*. Upon seeing me, Phoosie recalled the success of American golfers in Great Britain. As a boy, with his father, he had witnessed Walter Hagen winning the Open at Muirfield in 1928 and Bobby Jones winning the Open at Hoylake in 1930, the year of the famous "grand slam." I replied that I certainly wasn't in the class of those golfers, but I hoped to make a good showing in the Gnomewood tournament.

Geoff Cloverjoy remarked that he had taken some kidding about his "fanning the air" on his tee shot on the first hole last year. He joked that he had acquired the nickname "Whiffy." I said the term also applied to American baseball when a batter swings at the ball and misses. Geoff replied that a sportswriter in London had heard the expression watching American servicemen play baseball and applied it to golf.

Dick walked into the dining room, spotted us, and said, "Hi, Whiffy. How's your game?"

We all laughed, including Geoff, and he answered that he had been taking lessons from Si Bumbry and was making steady progress. This brought a few more laughs. Seriously, Geoff said he had taken several lessons from Hylton Barleycroft, Byford's brother, who is a well-respected teacher, and he looked forward to making a good showing in this year's tournament.

The menus arrived, and after placing our orders, we went across the hall to the Bear & Owl for a quick drink. When dinner arrived, we ate with a minimum of small talk. We all were eager to get to bed early.

CHAPTER 14

I awoke the next morning with a feeling of anticipation and mild apprehension about what the day would bring. I felt confident that whoever I was paired with would be delighted to have me as a partner. However, I had written numerous times about golf tournaments in which a player could shoot a sixty-four one day and a seventy-six the next. A gust of wind, a seemingly perfect drive that ends in a divot, or an unseen pebble on the putting green can drive a score in the wrong direction.

At breakfast, Dick waved to me to join him and Phil Frogwell-Potts at their table. Frogwell-Potts congratulated me on my qualifying score. I thanked him and told him I was looking forward to today's competition. He added that he wasn't sure how comfortable a professional in Great Britain would feel playing with an American since he understood foursomes were not a common form of competition in the States. Play in Britain used a slightly smaller golf ball. I told him I had been practicing with the smaller British ball and found the few extra yards it provided to be helpful.

At the next table, Fowler Thistletoe leaned over and asked us who might be paired with Miss Shotwell. "If it's a pro, we might as well give them the trophy and go home." Dick answered that Sir Harold had told him before the tournament that she would play in the professional ranks—just as she did in qualifying. In his opinion, it might be Mel Camberwick, an outstanding golfer at university with a ten handicap. Thistletoe said he thought Phogg-Smythe, assuming he wore his colorful purple attire, might be an attractive partner for Miss Shotwell. Then, glancing at Geoff Cloverjoy at a nearby table, he said he didn't think Geoff would make a good partner for her. We agreed, recalling how he had smacked her with his golf glove when she had fainted after seeing the body part in the bunker last year. Opinions were divided at our table as to whether she would recall this bizarre event and how it might affect her play this year. Dick said he was sure Sir Harold would not pair Miss Shotwell with Geoff.

We finished breakfast and had time for a cigarette before the bus arrived. When it did, we traveled to the Foggy Shores and picked up Giles Nippengay, Tommy Sapwood, and Byf Barleycroft. Byf was wearing his traditional red slacks. He glanced at the sportswriters contingent and shook his head. Geoff stirred in his seat as though he was about to say something, but he remained silent.

Arriving at the links, I noted several players already on the practice range. Judging from the size of their golf bags, these were professionals who would have caddies. On the ground beside the bags were several clubs the pros had been using to determine which seven would provide the best scoring opportunities.

In the clubhouse, Bob Paltry, Ian Crankshaw, and Colin Feathershanks were having an early whiskey, probably to settle their nerves. A notice pinned on the bulletin board by the bar stated that the pairings and starting times would be posted around nine fifteen. My anxiety rose. Two professionals, Bullwick Hawkshaw and Winston Peebles, were standing by the large map of the Gnomewood Links, taking turns pointing to certain holes they had found troublesome during qualifying.

Dick motioned to me to step outside on the veranda to avoid the nervous chatter in the clubhouse. We both felt this would reduce our anxiety. The sun was breaking through the morning mist, and the light breeze off the sea was refreshing. Dick estimated the breeze to be about ten miles per hour and would likely increase during the day. I saw several players come off the practice range and proceed to the practice putting green. They must have assumed they would have an early starting time. I glanced at my watch, saw that it was 9:10, and told Dick we should go back inside to wait for Sir Harold. I realized Miss Shotwell was nowhere to be seen and mentioned it to Dick. He reminded me that she was staying at Excelsior House with Sir Harold and his wife and would very likely arrive with Sir Harold.

At nine fifteen, the sound of the jeep outside the clubhouse indicated we were about to find out our fate for the next three days. Sir Harold and Miss Shotwell stepped out of the jeep and entered the clubhouse. Everyone rushed to the bulletin board to see their partners and starting times.

Miss Shotwell looked around the room, saw me, and moved through the crowd of golfers. "Hi, Mr. Nelson. We're partners."

For a few seconds, I was too stunned to answer, but then I recovered enough to say how pleased and relieved I was to join her—and that I hoped my game would hold up during the tournament.

She smiled and said we were leading off the tournament and should get our clubs and move to the practice range.

On the range, I felt a bit intimidated to be hitting balls beside her. Several players with later starting times, plus a few spectators, were gathered to where we were starting to practice. While admiring her swing, I heard several observers make less than favorable remarks about my efforts. I had been hitting wedge shots and would soon move up to irons and driver.

While practicing with my driver, I noted that Miss Shotwell was outdriving me by at least twenty yards—but I couldn't let it bother me. She was hitting the ball straight, which was reassuring. I thought we had a good chance of winning today's match. During a brief pause in her practice, I let her examine my 5-wood and encouraged her to hit a few balls with it. She admired the finish on it before commencing to hit. After several practice swings, she proceeded to hit half a dozen balls. Her shots traveled some twenty yards beyond what I had hit, using the 5-wood. She thanked me, and I thought if I could hit shots 200–219 yards with this club, we'd be a formidable team.

It was nearing our starting time, and as we walked to the practice green, Miss Shotwell asked which ball we should use. I said I was using a Dunlap 66, and she replied that she was using the Dunlap Maxflow. I said we should use her ball because that was what she had been using prior to the tournament. I didn't think using the Maxflow would make much difference. We agreed on this decision and discussed how to address each other.

She said, "Call me Sissy or just Sis—all my friends do."

I felt grateful and appreciative of this level of informality and said, "Call me John, but if you like the term 'Yank,' that's OK with me."

She replied, "John it is." She also mentioned that she would be carrying her own bag.

We practiced putting for a few minutes and headed to the first tee. I noticed our opponents putting before heading to the first tee. Mel Camberwick and the pro Reggie Turnbuckle were sinking their putts, and I realized we were in for a tough match.

CHAPTER 15

On the first tee, we shook hands with our opponents. They were delighted to meet Miss Shotwell and welcomed the opportunity to compete against her. A small gallery had assembled, and although not advertised, word had spread about Sir Harold's tournament. Among the gallery was a sallow-faced man with a notebook. He was wearing a black peaked hat and mismatched suit. Dick had mentioned him to me at breakfast as someone to avoid. He wrote under the name of Wallace Picklewood for the *Sports World Insider*, which focused on various scandals in the sports world, real or imagined.

Dick had said, "If you happen to see a copy, don't read it. As an American, you may be in his report of this tournament—and it won't be flattering."

On the tee, Sir Harold welcomed the players and handed out scorecards and a sheet defining the vegetable-growing areas that were to be played as "ground under repair."

Sir Harold said, "If a shot lands in one of these areas, the ball should be retrieved and dropped within one club length from the green-and-white stake marking the drop zone. If the ball appears to have landed in the vegetables but cannot be found without trampling on the vegetables, another ball is to be dropped by the green and white stake without penalty."

Miss Shotwell was up first. She was wearing a yellow sweater, a dark blue skirt, and tan-and-white golf shoes. The starter, Harley Bellows, resplendent in red blazer and light blue slacks, introduced her as one of the outstanding young lady golfers in the British Isles and winner of the recent Midlands Lady Amateur Championship. There was brief applause as she nodded to the gallery and then teed up her ball. After a quick practice swing, she blasted a drive of some 240 yards down the middle.

Reggie Turnbuckle was next to hit. He smacked a drive of about the same length as Miss Shotwell's, down the left side of the fairway. I felt a sense of relief that we were off to a good start even though I hadn't hit a shot.

We parred the first hole—and so did our opponents. The second hole was also halved with par. I hit a good drive left-center that left Miss Shotwell with an easy iron shot to the green. However, I didn't sink the short putt for a birdie. Moving on, I hoped we could take advantage of the par-5 third hole with a birdie. It was up to me to hit our second shot that would set up Sis for a wedge shot that would result in a short putt for a birdie. Both Camberwick and I hit wobbly second shots, leaving our partners with midirons to the green. Ultimately, both teams took two putts for par.

The fourth hole, a par-3, was halved with bogies. I pulled my tee shot into the bunker guarding the left side of the green, and Camberwick drove into the bunker behind the green. The bunker shots by our partners left putts in the ten-foot range that we failed to sink. The resulting short putts were conceded.

The fifth hole was halved with par, and it was on to the troublesome sixth hole. Sis and I decided I would hit my drive toward the right side of the fairway where it bent left. If my ball should land in the carrots, that wouldn't be a problem. Consequently, I teed my ball on the left side of the tee and aimed at the right side of the fairway. I hit one of my better drives that landed on the right side of the fairway and rolled into the carrots.

"Good drive," Sis said.

Camberwick and Turnbuckle had the same strategy. I watched Camberwick fiddle with his grip, appearing to open the clubface slightly before addressing the ball. He then blasted a monster drive that sliced over the carrots and landed in relatively deep rough.

As we walked to our respective tee shots, I thought we had an advantage. Sis easily retrieved my tee shot from the carrots and dropped it one club length from the green-and-white stake. It took our opponents several minutes to find Camberwick's drive. Sis walked over to where their ball lay nestled in deep rough. She returned to me and said, "It's deep."

Turnbuckle took several practice swings before blasting a wedge shot to the fairway well short of the green. Miss Shotwell then struck an 8-iron onto the green, about ten feet from the flagstick. Camberwick played a wedge from the fairway to fifteen feet from the flagstick.

Turnbuckle was first to putt. He missed on the low side of the hole, and we conceded their bogie attempt. I had a birdie putt, but Sis said to leave it short so it didn't roll too far by the hole. I did just that, leaving her a putt of about six inches. Our opponents conceded the putt and the hole. Miss Shotwell and I were 1-up.

The seventh hole was halved with bogies. Camberwick and I each hit the second shots into the bunker guarding the right side of the green. Our partners' explosion shots from the bunker avoided the flagstick, leaving putts of some fifteen feet that we failed to sink.

The eighth hole, a par-3, was halved with par, and it was on to the ninth hole, a 525-yard par-5. Miss Shotwell was first up and drove into the eggplants along the right side of the fairway. Turnbuckle then hammered a drive of some 260 yards in the fairway. I approached the eggplants and found my ball. Dropping it near the stake, I hit my 5-wood about two hundred yards to the fairway.

Camberwick was next to play. He slammed a 3-wood down the fairway to about one hundred yards short of the green. Miss Shotwell was away and played a 6-iron to the green. Turnbuckle then struck a low-running wedge to the green that failed to check up, leaving Camberwick with a thirty-footer for birdie. He was short by about three feet. I had a putt of about ten feet that I ran by the left lip of the hole, leaving a two-foot putt for par. Our opponents failed to concede this putt. After Turnbuckle lined up the three-footer and sank it, they conceded our short putt. We remained 1-up.

Starting the back nine holes, we paused briefly for refreshments before starting on hole 10. This hole is 404 yards slight dogleg right, with a large fairway bunker guarding the right side of the fairway where it bends right. Sis advised me to aim left-center and, if my drive should land in the lentils, the angle to the green would be better. I took her advice and drove just short of the lentils but still in the fairway. Our opponents had the same strategy, and both teams were successful in parring the hole.

The eleventh hole, a 212-yard par-3, played into the wind, which had increased over the past hour. Miss Shotwell was first to play. She struck a 3-wood with a three-quarter swing. The shot came off perfectly, and the ball landed just short of the green, rolling about ten feet short of the flagstick. The small gallery following us applauded.

Turnbuckle was now up. He chose a 3-iron and stroked a shot that I thought would land on the green, but it faded in the wind and landed short of the green, in the lettuce. Arriving at the green, Camberwick removed their ball from the lettuce and dropped it in the surrounding rough. He had a difficult chip shot because the pin was on the right—and the green sloped to the right.

After several practice swings, he struck a chip that barely missed the flagstick and rolled some twenty feet beyond. Turnbuckle now had a twenty-foot putt for par. He struck a good putt that barely missed the hole, and we conceded their remaining short putt.

I had a ten-foot putt that broke from right to left. Sis and I surveyed it before she pointed to where the putt would break and said to try to leave it short. I followed her advice and putted to about a foot from the cup. Our opponents conceded this short putt, and we were now 2-up.

Holes twelve and thirteen were halved, and it was on to fourteen, a 517-yard par-5. On the tee, we decided the main trouble was on the left, where three bunkers guarded a dogleg. The mustard growth on the right was less troublesome—should a drive land there—and I took one practice swing and belted a 240-yard drive down the middle.

Camberwick, not to be outdone, hammered a drive some 260 yards down the left side of the fairway. Miss Shotwell had the next shot. She hit a 3-wood that caught the breeze and fell about eighty yards short of the green. Turnbuckle followed with a 3-wood that landed and rolled to about twenty yards short of the green. I realized I would have to hit a wedge shot to six or eight feet or better from the flagstick to give us a reasonable chance at a birdie. I struck a wedge about ten feet from the flagstick—not bad—but I had hoped to be closer.

Camberwick was next to play. He selected a wedge for the twenty-yard pitch shot. He must have been feeling some pressure, being 2-down, because he swung and took a large divot, the ball advancing to the edge of the green. A series of oaths followed. I hoped Sis didn't catch all the words, but I suppose, playing on occasion with men, such language is not unexpected. Turnbuckle now had a twenty-five-foot putt for birdie. He stroked a putt that was online but stopped just short of the hole. We conceded this short putt. Sis now had a ten-foot putt that broke slightly to the right. She stood over the ball for several seconds, then stroked the putt into the hole for a 3-up lead.

We halved the fifteenth hole and moved on to the sixteenth, a 400-yard par-4. I was on the tee and smacked a 230-yard drive down the middle. Camberwick followed with a drive of about 250 yards. Walking down the fairway, I saw Sis would have an iron shot of some 170 yards. We discussed the distance, and she feared her 6-iron wasn't quite enough club to reach the green—and the 3-iron was too much. I reminded her that on the eleventh hole, she had gripped down on a 3-wood with success, but she said she felt confident with that shot and thought the 3-iron was still too much club. She finally decided she would hit a strong 6-iron. The breeze was behind us, and if the ball landed just short of the green, I would have an easy chip shot to the flagstick and avoid the risk of hitting long and the ball landing in the deep bunker behind the green.

She hit a 6-iron that was just short of the green, and as we walked to the ball, she said, "Chip it in, partner."

Turnbuckle had the next shot. He slammed a midiron that rode the wind, landed on the back of the green, and trickled off into the back bunker. Camberwick would now have a difficult bunker shot, which had to clear the high lip of the bunker and not roll too far from the flagstick when it landed. I approached my chip shot and selected an 8-iron to play a chip and run.

Meanwhile, Camberwick had entered the bunker. I could barely see the top of his cap as he took several practice swings and then blasted the ball up—only to have it land on the edge of the bunker and trickle back in. He started to address the ball, but Turnbuckle reminded him it was his shot. Turnbuckle addressed the ball, dug in his feet to secure his stance, and blasted the ball up and out, the ball landing some fifteen feet from the flagstick.

It was my shot, and I saw what I thought was a clear path to the hole. I struck what I thought was a shot right online—it was—but it stopped five feet short of the hole. I was disgusted with myself and apologized to Sis, but she reminded me that Camberwick had a bogie putt. If he missed, we had two putts to win the hole.

Camberwick and Turnbuckle lined up the fifteen-footer, and then Camberwick struck a putt that rolled several inches by the hole. Sis started to address our par putt before our opponents conceded the hole and the match.

We shook hands with our opponents and congratulated them on their play. I was tempted to give Miss Shotwell a big hug, but I thought a handshake would be more appropriate. We hadn't walked more than a few steps back toward the clubhouse before a man in a pointed hat stepped in our path and introduced himself as Wallace Picklewood, a sports reporter. He quickly remarked how much my poor play accentuated Miss Shotwell's superlative golf. Sis and her younger sister, who had been following our match, hurried around Picklewood and walked quickly to the clubhouse. I kept the reporter's attention by saying how our opponents' play brought out our best play.

As Picklewood turned to where Camberwick and Turnbuckle had been standing, they scooted away toward the clubhouse before he could interview them. Picklewood then jotted down a few notes before turning around and looking for other contestants to interview.

I slung my clubs over my shoulder and walked back to the clubhouse.

Sis and Rose were resting in the wicker chairs on the veranda. "Isn't he something?" Sis remarked. "He cornered me after a junior tournament in Aylesford and told me how my game matched my immature appearance. It upset me briefly until I realized I had played well enough and was runner-up."

I reassured her that no reputable publication would publish his tripe, but I later found out this wasn't necessarily so.

Sir Harold drove up in his new electric-powered golf cart and offered to drive us to watch some of the matches in progress. I declined as I needed a beer and some rest, but Sis and Rosie were eager to ride in his cart. They rode off with Sir Harold to the fourteenth tee.

After obtaining a beer, I settled in a chair on the veranda and gazed out on the back nine. Walking in were Paltry and Fossilgrass, followed by Marsden and Quickfoot. Marsden spotted me and walked over to congratulate me on our victory. Word had spread that we had won. He then related his team's loss. He said, "Quickfoot was off his game, and we were never able to gain the lead. If we played well enough for par, so did Paltry and Fossilgrass. A few bogies did us in. We gradually fell behind and finally lost three and two."

I asked facetiously if Paltry's bright yellow attire had bothered him.

He replied, "It brightened the match."

With that, he headed for the bar.

Several other groups were walking in and turning in their results. I knew Paltry and Fossilgrass were winners. Frogwell-Potts and his pro partner, Winston Peebles, had defeated Crankshaw and Sapwood. Cloverjoy and Nippengay were victorious over Thinwood and Suggs. Dick and his partner, Harry Vardon Taylor, were still on the course.

On the seventeenth tee, I saw the bright red slacks of one of Dick's opponents, Byf Barleycroft. Byf was first up, which meant he and his partner, Phogg-Smythe, were likely leading. Barleycroft powered his usual long drive down the fairway, and Taylor hit a constrained low fade to the edge of the spinach. Barleycroft's drive was about forty yards farther down the fairway.

When it was Dick's turn to hit, he stroked a 3-wood that landed about ten yards short of the green. Phogg-Smythe smacked a 3-iron that landed on the lower edge of the green about twenty feet from the flagstick. Dick and his partner walked to where Dick's 3-wood landed. From there, Taylor decided to hit a wedge to the flag. He lofted a shot that ran some ten feet by the hole, leaving Dick with a difficult sidehill putt for par. Barleycroft now had a twelve-foot putt for birdie. He stroked a putt that stopped just short of the hole. This was conceded.

Dick needed to sink his ten-footer to save par. He stroked a putt that appeared to be online, but it veered off and missed the edge of the hole.

That was the end of the match. Phogg-Smythe and Barleycroft won two and one. The two teams shook hands and headed for the clubhouse.

I met Dick as he approached the clubhouse. I said I was sorry he and Taylor lost—and that Miss Shotwell and I had looked forward to possibly competing against them at some point in the tournament.

Dick shook his head. "We didn't play well—and, on several holes, Barleycroft sank putts of over twenty feet to save par. Then we bogied ten and thirteen, the par-3 holes, to fall behind, and we never caught up." He and Harry Vardon Taylor headed for the bar.

I turned my attention back to the sixteenth hole. A figure was descending into the deep bunker behind the green. Dr. Middlefield and his partner, Fowler Thistletoe, were standing off to the side and watching their opponents. The player in the bunker took several practice swings and then drilled the ball into the side of the bunker directly in front of him. I recognized the player in the bunker as the partner of Hamilton Smart. He climbed down into the bunker to play the next shot and quickly surveyed the situation before retrieving the ball, taking a penalty stroke and back-of-the-line relief, and dropping the ball. After two practice swings, he blasted the ball out about twenty feet from the flagstick. On the green, Hamilton Smart saw the doctor and Thistletoe were about ten feet from a birdie and conceded the hole and the match.

Back at the clubhouse, I met the four who had just finished their match. Dr. Middlefield asked how Miss Shotwell and I had done, and I told him we were winners. He remarked that he wasn't surprised.

Thistletoe complimented the doctor on maintaining his composure when he was about to putt as a spectator yelled, "Fill that cavity, Doc!"

The doctor commented that he had heard this before during tournaments and found it amusing.

We joined those in the clubhouse who were having a beverage and talking over the day's results. Dick had just finished a beer and was ordering a second. He asked me how Miss Shotwell had played. Before I could answer, Camberwick and Turnbuckle answered by praising her poise and ability. Turnbuckle said he outdrove her on several holes, but she seemed unfazed and never forced a shot.

Byf Barleycroft overheard our conversation and interjected that he questioned the wisdom of inviting Miss Shotwell to compete at Gnomewood. He thought her game would not hold up during this tournament—and she would be a drag on her playing partner. I told Barleycroft that I was aware of the quality of her play in amateur competitions, and she had been paired with men in local club tournaments since she was twelve. Barleycroft answered that he hoped Miss Shotwell and I would meet them in competition later in the tournament.

Sir Harold and Leffingwell were huddled in a corner. After a few minutes, they proceeded to the bulletin board where they posted the results for today and scheduled tomorrow's matches. Miss Shotwell and I would be competing against Bob Paltry and Hew Fossilgrass. In other matches, Cloverjoy and Nippengay were facing Marblehead and Feathershanks; Frogwell-Potts and Peebles versus Phogg-Smythe and Barleycroft; and Thistletoe and Dr. Middlefield against Quigley and Dedmon.

The conversation resumed at a higher pitch as the teams discussed their plans for tomorrow. The doctor downed his second whiskey and soda and waved goodbye to the crowd as he exited for the parking lot. I was ready to leave also. Miss Shotwell had warned me not to stay up too late with the sportswriters. The bus had pulled up to the clubhouse after having driven the pros and caddies to the Foggy Shores, and I told Dick I would see him back at the Prince Rupert.

On the bus, Thistletoe amused us with some of the random comments Dr. Middlefield had made during play. He said he couldn't stand Bumly's hat with the fishing lures and his lunging golf swing.

He wondered if Phogg-Smythe, who was on the bus, ever changed his purple attire. Phogg-Smythe overheard the remark and answered that he had several pairs of purple sweaters and pants. He wondered the same about Barleycroft's red slacks. "Does he ever change them?" Since Phogg-Smythe was Barleycroft's partner, he said he would ask him tomorrow. He added that—with his purple outfit and Barleycroft's red slacks—they would make a colorful team.

Arriving at the Prince Rupert, several writers made a dash for the Bear & Owl. I decided to head for the dining room, and I shared the dinner table with Derick Marblehead and Ian Crankshaw. Ian said he wished he had spent more time on the range, following the posting of the schedule. That way, his pro partner, Tommy Sapwood, could have spent more time evaluating Ian's swing and discussing their strategy on certain holes before they teed off. Other criticisms followed.

Derick suggested pairing the top professional with the lowest writer who qualified. This might even out the field. I ventured that this might discourage some pros from competing. I couldn't imagine the doctor being paired with Bumbrey. Ian offered the idea that the pros might be given the opportunity, before the tournament started, to choose their partners from among the writers they have known in the past. This might stimulate the writers to sharpen their games before the tournament. I cautioned that some pros might start "grooming" certain sportswriters whom they knew would be competing. We all agreed we should bring these ideas to Sir Harold after tomorrow's matches.

Over dessert, I asked about the new professionals in this year's tournament, David Knibbles and Winston Peebles. Ian had observed them in the Great Northern Masters and recalled they had been contenders. He also had followed Peebles during Open qualifying last year and said he was a long hitter, but his short game let him down. He thought they were a good addition to this year's Gnomewood tournament.

After dessert, Ian and Derick joined Christopher Thinwood, Frogwell-Potts, and Pat Quigley in the Bear & Owl for what Ian called some "ancient Scotch whiskey." I respectfully declined and started to return to my room as Dick and three young sports reporters entered the dining room. I gathered they had gone to the Rake & Dibble to discuss the first day's play and not be overheard by those competing in the tournament, including myself.

Dick introduced me as Miss Shotwell's partner, which they already knew from the day's play. The reporters immediately said they would love to interview her. Dick restrained their enthusiasm and said she was not staying at the Prince Rupert, but they could interview her after tomorrow's match. I thought it wise for Dick not to say she was staying at Excelsior House for fear of their descending on Sir Harold and demanding to interview Miss Shotwell.

I spoke up and said that, as Miss Shotwell's partner, I would be part of the interview. One of them started to ask me about competing with her as a partner, but I said I would talk to them tomorrow. As I turned to walk to my room, I told Dick I would see him tomorrow, adding I was sorry his partner hadn't lived up to his name.

As I passed the lobby, I saw a television report on tomorrow's weather. It wasn't reassuring with predictions of intermittent squalls and winds of ten to fifteen miles per hour. I assumed Miss Shotwell had played in that type of weather before.

In my room, I reviewed my notes on today's play and my impression of our opponents tomorrow. Bob Paltry was a long hitter but tended to slice. Assuming the pro teed off first on the first hole, Paltry would tee off first on the even-numbered holes, and a slice on several of these holes could leave his partner, Fossilgrass, with a difficult second shot. Fossilgrass had a good all-around game, but I didn't know how skilled he was at playing from deep grass or bunkers. I knew he was recognized as a skilled putter; his experience as a greenskeeper enabled him to read greens better than the average professional. I concluded I would make Miss Shotwell's next shot easier if I could drive my tee shots in the fairway. With that, I showered and went to bed.

CHAPTER 16

Morning brought the predicted rain and wind. I donned my weatherproof outfit and went to the dining room. I shared a table with Fowler Thistletoe and Phil Frogwell-Potts. After we shed part of our rain gear, both writers expressed interest in my impression of Miss Shotwell. I replied she was an excellent golfer who elevated my game.

Frogwell-Potts said, "If my partner and I win our match today, we will meet in the semifinals."

I replied, "Miss Shotwell and I will be looking forward to the competition."

Thistletoe was frequently glancing at the entryway, and I suspected he was looking for his partner, Dr. Middlefield. I casually mentioned that if he was looking for his partner, he would find him on the practice range. I reminded Thistletoe that Dick Whistle had been paired with the doctor last year, and Dick told me the dentist would appear shortly before their tee time. Dick suspected the doctor warmed up at a nearby course, arriving at Gnomewood for a brief practice before tee time.

We finished breakfast, put on our rain gear, and boarded the bus for the links. Upon arrival, I headed for my locker, took out my clubs, and walked to the practice range. Thistletoe accompanied me, and since the doctor hadn't arrived yet, he retreated to the clubhouse.

Miss Shotwell hadn't appeared either, but I wanted to start practicing. The mist limited visibility to slightly less than three hundred yards, which was just enough to allow practice. I started hitting balls and watched the ball falling about five yards short of what I would have expected under normal conditions. I worked my way up to my driver and saw the ball disappearing into the haze that was settling on the links. I suspected there might be a delay in starting.

126

Our opponents, Bob Paltry and Hew Fossilgrass, arrived and started practicing. I couldn't believe what Paltry was wearing. He wore a black golf sweater, a yellow rain jacket, mustard yellow plus fours, and black-and-yellow striped stockings. He looked like someone going to a costume party dressed as a bumblebee. I paused to watch the pair hit, and both were long hitters. As I expected, Paltry was slicing about one out of three drives. He didn't appear to be correcting this flaw. Fossilgrass, despite what appeared to be too upright a swing, dropped the club in the proper slot as he started the downswing and was hitting long, straight drives that disappeared into the haze. They would be formidable opponents.

After watching Paltry and Fossilgrass for a few minutes, I walked to the putting green. A layer of moisture on the surface would influence the roll, and I had forgotten to bring a towel to wipe off the ball and face of the putter.

I went to the clubhouse to get a towel and saw Sis and Rosie drinking hot cocoa. They were both wearing yellow rain gear and said they were ready for a cold, damp day on the links. I brought up an idea I had been mulling over in my mind. "Would it be to our advantage to have me tee off first. You would tee off first on the even-numbered holes—and on holes 14, 16, and maybe 18—an advantage if the match is close or tied."

She thought for a few seconds and said, "Holes 3, 7, 9, and 17 require a relatively long tee shot." She agreed to my idea, but I detected a hint of doubt in her response. She and Rose finished their cocoa, said they would see me later, and walked to the practice range.

The putting green was drying, and I started to practice. I knew the greens on the links would speed up as the day progressed. I noted an increasing number of spectators gathering by the first tee and surmised that news of the tournament was gaining interest.

After about fifteen minutes, Sis and Rose joined me on the putting green. We had agreed to continue playing the Dunlap Maxflow, as we did yesterday, and we continued to practice putting until it was near ten o'clock, our tee time.

On the tee, Harley Bellows was set to announce who would hit first. He seemed surprised that I would lead off our team instead of Miss Shotwell. He chuckled and said he hoped to introduce an attractive lady golfer, who was well known in amateur tournaments, and he asked who I was.

I replied, "A sportswriter from New York here at the invitation of Sir Harold Gilroy."

He said he would keep that in mind.

Dick approached Miss Shotwell and me and wished us good luck, and then he noted I had pulled the driver from my bag. He questioned why I was leading off, and I gave him my reasons. He thought for several seconds, said, "An interesting idea," and walked away. I was left with the impression that he didn't think it was such a good idea.

A minute later, the mellifluous voice of Harley Bellows announced the start of the day's matches. He emphasized the strong field that would be competing today and then introduced "a sportswriter from New York, who is paired today with Miss Forsythia Shotwell, an outstanding young lady golfer."

The applause was muted, I suspect, because the spectators were looking forward to Miss Shotwell leading off.

I tipped my visor to acknowledge the applause and teed up my ball. The knot in my stomach grew tighter as I took several practice swings, addressed the ball, and fired away. My drive had a slight fade that the breeze pushed back toward the center of the fairway, about 220 yards out. I was relieved.

Next on the tee was Fossilgrass. He blasted a drive of some 250 yards down the middle, about thirty yards beyond my drive. I realized this would be the difference in our drives all day and tried not to let it bother me. I was just glad my drive was in the fairway, leaving Sis with a clear shot at the green.

As we walked down the fairway, I said to Sis that I hoped I hadn't placed her at a disadvantage with my being outdriven on the odd-numbered holes. She told me she was glad she was away and thought hitting first would be an advantage during the round. She proceeded to hit a 3-iron to the green.

The next shot was Paltry's, and he struck a midiron to about ten feet from the pin. On the green, I had about a twenty-foot putt that I left short. Fossilgrass sank a ten-footer for a birdie. We were 1-down.

Hole 2 was halved with pars. The third hole, a 503-yard par-5, required a good tee shot so Sis could use her 3-wood to move us to birdie range. Fossilgrass was first up and hammered a drive some 250 yards down the left side of the fairway. I managed to hit a drive of about 230 yards that landed in the beet patch.

Sis retrieved the ball and dropped it in the designated area. She then played a 3-wood to the fairway, leaving me with an 8-iron shot to the green. Paltry lined up his 3-wood and smacked a shot that landed about ten yards short of the green. The next shot was mine. I lofted an 8-iron that landed on the green and ran to about six feet from the flagstick. Fossilgrass played a chip shot that rolled to about two feet from the flag.

On the green, Sis lined up the six-footer and sank it for a birdie. Paltry walked around his two-foot putt before sinking it. He seemed a bit miffed that we didn't concede it, but the putt had a slight break, and Sis muttered to me not to concede it. We remained 1-down.

The fourth hole was a par-3 of 165 yards. Perhaps Paltry was still irritated by having to putt on the previous hole because he hit a poor tee shot that landed in the broccoli. Sis then hit a beautiful 6-iron to about five feet from the flag.

Fossilgrass now had a wedge shot from the drop area, where the rough was three or four inches deep, and he blasted the ball out to about ten feet from the flag.

I had a five-footer for birdie that I just missed on the right. The tap-in for par was conceded. Paltry spent a minute lining up his par putt with the help of his partner and stroked a putt that missed by several inches. The score was even.

The fifth hole was halved with par, and it was on to the difficult sixth hole. I was glad Sis was teeing off first. She hit a beautiful, controlled draw to where the dogleg bent left, leaving me with a straight shot to the green. Paltry, hoping not to be outdriven by a lady competitor, struck one of his spectacular slices that faded into the rough beyond the carrots. It took several minutes to find Paltry's drive. A spectator had seen where the ball entered the high rough.

Fossilgrass had to play a wedge out to the fairway, leaving his partner about sixty yards from the green. I had the next shot. I stroked a 8-iron that landed about twenty feet from the flagstick. Paltry had the next shot, and he hit a wedge that landed on the edge of the green. Fossilgrass was away, and he chipped to about two feet from the cup. That was their fourth shot. Sis now had a twenty-foot putt for birdie that just missed, leaving me a tap-in for par. Thus, we won the hole and were 1-up.

The seventh hole, a 430-yard par-4, was halved with bogies. Fossilgrass and I hit weak drives, and our partners hit their approach shots into one of the pot bunkers guarding the right side of the green. The resulting bunker shots left long par putts that were missed.

The short eighth hole was halved with par. I was first up on the ninth hole, a par-5 of 525 yards, and in my eagerness to hit a long drive, I topped my shot that bounced down the fairway about two hundred yards. Fossilgrass then hammered his drive some 260 yards down the middle.

The next shot was Mis Shotwell's. She hit a 3-wood some 230 yards that landed in a bunker guarding the left side of the fairway.

Paltry then addressed his partner's drive. He smacked a 3-wood to about forty yards short of the green. I was now faced with a long bunker shot of about one hundred yards that I played with an 8-iron. My shot landed well short of the green. Miss Shotwell followed with a pitch shot that landed about six feet from the flag. Fossilgrass was next to hit. He lofted a wedge shot that landed about four feet from the flag. I was away and had the six-footer for par. There was a slight right to left break that I misjudged, resulting in a bogie. Paltry sank a birdie putt of four feet, winning the hole and squaring the match.

Dick was waiting for me on the tenth tee. I told him my poor drive had cost us the hole, and he encouraged me to stay calm and not let the previous hole bother me. He pointed out that there were several holes on the back nine where Paltry would likely find trouble off the tee, leaving Fossilgrass with a difficult second shot. I thanked him for his advice and walked over to the refreshment cart. Sis and I had apple juice and a cookie. She also offered advice on keeping calm and not worrying about Fossilgrass outdriving me. Our opponents chose beer for their refreshment.

The sun had emerged from the mist, and we shed all our rain gear. Paltry now looked like what I regarded as his bumblebee outfit.

"Go sting 'um, Bobby," someone yelled.

Obviously, I wasn't the only one who saw him as a bee.

Paltry looked over at the gallery to see if he could identify the source of the remark. I suspected it was one of the young sports reporters who had been on the train from London and stopped at the Rake & Dibble for a pint or two before coming to the links. Hopefully, they would have some sense of decorum during the match.

The tenth hole was a slight dogleg right, with a large bunker where the fairway begins to bend. To the right of the bunker was a large lentil growth. Paltry was on the tee. After two vigorous practice swings, he belted a drive that sliced into the lentils.

Miss Shotwell was now on the tee. She elected to hit a 3-wood and drove down the middle about 230 yards. Fossilgrass had to retrieve his partner's drive from the lentils and drop near the stake marking the drop zone. The grass was thick because of the moisture from the sea spray. He attempted to hit a midiron from the grass, but the shot landed well short of the green. I then had a 6-iron to the green that landed about fifteen feet from the flagstick. Paltry then played a wedge shot that landed about twenty feet from the flagstick, leaving his partner with a par putt. Fossilgrass missed the putt, and we took two putts for par and the win. Sis and I were 1-up.

We halved the eleventh hole, a 212-yard par-3 that played into the breeze. I used my 5-wood off the tee and came up short. Fossilgrass hit a 3-iron that landed on the back edge of the green. Both teams were able to get down in par.

The twelfth hole was halved, and it was on to the thirteenth. On the par-3 thirteenth hole, the deep bunker behind the green led to both teams hitting short of the green. Excellent chip shots resulted in easy par putts.

We moved on to the 517-yard fourteenth hole that was playing into the wind. I recalled the body parts being found in the general vicinity and hoped Miss Shotwell would not recall this macabre scene. She was on the tee and blasted a drive some 240 yards down the right edge of the fairway. I felt relieved.

Paltry was on the tee and again, I think, trying to outdrive a lady golfer, he smashed a ballooning drive that faded into the mustard growth. I thought briefly about suggesting he hit a provisional ball—if his ball had bounced out of the mustard and landed in deep rough—but I thought this might be interpreted as gamesmanship and didn't want to leave any hard feelings.

We walked to where Sis's drive landed, and I chose a 5-wood for my next shot. I had a good lie and struck a solid shot that landed within an easy wedge shot to the green. As I suspected, Paltry and Fossilgrass had difficulty finding Paltry's drive. Several spectators pointed to an area outside the mustard. Fossilgrass knew if your ball was not easily found in the vegetables and the player was reasonably certain the shot had landed there, they could take a drop by the stake in the drop zone without penalty.

Fossilgrass was about to drop his ball by the stake, but Miss Shotwell and I objected to this and said we should question the spectators as to where they thought the tee shot had landed.

After further searching, Paltry's drive was found. Fossilgrass now had to play from rough about three inches thick. He selected a 3-wood, which I didn't think was a wise choice, and blasted ball and turf out onto the fairway. Paltry then hit a midiron into a pot bunker along the left side of the fairway. From there, Fossilgrass lofted a sand-iron to about ten feet from the flag.

Sis was next to play and struck a wedge to about eight feet from the flag.

Paltry now had a ten-foot sidehill putt that broke to the right. This was their fifth shot. His putt broke a foot below the hole.

I now had a birdie putt, but after Sis warned me about being too aggressive, I nudged the putt to about six inches from the cup. This tap-in was conceded, and we were now 2-up.

The short fifteenth hole, a par-3, was halved with par, and we moved to the sixteenth, a par-4 playing downwind. The main hazard on this hole was a large, deep bunker behind the green created by a German bomb. There was also a bunker among the potatoes growing along the right side of the fairway.

Miss Shotwell was first on the tee. Because the hole was playing downwind, she elected to hit a 3-wood off the tee and avoid the potatoes and the bunker. Her drive traveled about 230 yards down the middle. Paltry, not to be outdone, laced a drive of some 270 yards down the right side of the fairway. I now had a shot of about 160 yards to the green. I used my 6-iron, which was an ideal club for me to hit 160 yards. After Sis warned me about the deep bunker behind the green, I gripped down about an inch on the 6-iron. The shot came off as planned, landing at the base of the green.

Fossilgrass was now up. He sensed an opportunity to birdie the hole if he could hit his wedge close to the cup. Because of his enthusiasm and the fact that he was hitting downwind, he blasted his wedge to the back of the green and then over the side—and into the "Nazi crater."

After marking our ball, Sis and I walked to the back of the green to see what shot Paltry would have from the bottom of the bunker. Paltry stepped down to where the ball had landed, wedge in hand, and Fossilgrass stood by the edge of the bunker and instructed his partner to open the clubface and swing hard. He took several vigorous practice strokes and then swung hard, and the ball emerged from a cloud of sand, landing at the top of the bunker. It stayed there for a second, and then it rolled back to the bottom of the bunker.

In frustration—and before Fossilgrass could stop him—Paltry swung again, exploding the ball out onto the green about twenty feet from the flagstick. Clearly, Paltry had played out of turn, and Fossilgrass should have played the second attempt to escape from the bunker. My impression of this event was that our opponents had lost the hole, but Fossilgrass maintained their ball should be replaced in the bunker and he would play the next stroke, their fourth, counting a one-stroke penalty.

Paltry retrieved their ball from the green and placed it in the bunker near where he had attempted to blast it out. Fossilgrass exploded the ball out to about ten feet from the flagstick.

Sis was away and had a putt of about twenty-five feet from the edge of the green. She putted the ball to about two feet below the cup.

Paltry was next to putt. His ten-footer for bogie rolled to the edge of the cup and then sank.

I had a two-foot putt that our opponents refused to concede. It was straight uphill.

Sis said, "Don't leave it short."

I stepped back, took a deep breath, and looked at the two-foot line again before sinking it. We won three and two! I felt a great sense of relief as I tipped my cap to the small gallery applauding our victory. Paltry and Fossilgrass offered tepid handshakes before we left the green and walked back to the clubhouse. I offered my appreciation to Sis for her advice and steady play. We both thought we won the hole when Paltry played out of turn.

Back in the clubhouse, Sir Harold was waiting for the first match to finish. Food and various beverages were waiting for us. There was also a plate of cookies for the ladies. Sis's little sister, Rosie, had joined the gallery at some point during the match. I grabbed a plate of sausages and cheese and a beer, and we moved out to the veranda to watch the incoming matches.

Fossilgrass walked over to where we were sitting and said they probably did lose the last hole when his partner played out of turn. He offered his congratulations to Miss Shotwell and said she could compete at a high level and hoped he would see her name competing in the Ladies Open. She thanked him, said she hoped to qualify, and wished him luck in his attempt to qualify for the Open. I looked for Paltry and saw that he had retreated to the practice range. He was easy to spot in his bumblebee outfit.

I spotted two players standing on the eighteenth green, Barleycroft and Phogg-Smythe. They remained there until Leffingwell, who had been following this match, motioned them to clear the green. There were players waiting to hit on the eighteenth fairway. The two appeared to be having an animated conversation as they walked to the clubhouse. They walked by us and headed to opposite ends of the bar. Phogg-Smythe joined several sportswriters for a beer, and Barleycroft ordered a double whiskey and, to no one in particular, spouted off about his partner's play and his "disgusting purple attire."

The team of Frogwell-Potts and Peebles had won their match against Barleycroft and Phogg-Smythe two up. This match had one controversial event when Frogwell-Potts and Phogg-Smythe mistakenly played their opponent's ball from the rough. The mistake wasn't discovered until the teams were on the green and ready to putt. After cleaning their ball, the mistake was discovered. Sir Harold was summoned, and after discussing the matter with the teams and glancing down the fairway and seeing players ready to hit, he ruled that the hole was halved and to play on. He emphasized the importance of marking their ball, particularly when playing the same brand. Sis was sure the first team to play—in this situation, it was Phogg-Smythe—made the initial mistake and should have lost the hole.

Frogwell-Potts and Peebles would be our opponents in the semifinals tomorrow. Miss Shotwell and I walked over to chat with them and said we looked forward to our match. Frogwell-Potts responded that they had heard nothing but good reports about us and anticipated our match tomorrow would be well attended. Golf fans were eager to see Miss Shotwell play. He glanced over his shoulder at Barleycroft at the bar and said their match had an acrimonious tone. Barleycroft was not in championship form, and he frequently criticized Phogg-Smythe. On two occasions, Barleycroft drove into the deep rough and had to declare a lost ball. Then he berated his partner for not spotting where the ball landed. Peebles added that he expected better sportsmanship from a fellow professional.

Miss Shotwell smiled and said, "John Nelson and I will be on our best behavior tomorrow."

Just then, Dick made his appearance. He had been following the match with Thistletoe and Dr. Middlefield against Quigley and Dedmon, and he wasn't surprised that the dentist and Thistletoe had won. The doctor was playing well and was supportive of Thistletoe.

Dick said he had heard Miss Shotwell and I were winners.

I said, "Our opponents seemed overly eager to show us up. Paltry seemed to think he had to outdrive Miss Shotwell at every opportunity, and his wild drives cost them several holes. On sixteen, Fossilgrass drove over the green and landed in the deep bunker behind the green. This left Paltry with a difficult sand shot that he failed to blast out. He then played out of turn, but they thought we settled the situation as Fossilgrass replayed the bunker shot. They lay three on the green, and Miss Shotwell and I parred the hole, thus winning the match. Fossilgrass and Paltry were a bit surly as we left the green, but Fossilgrass later came over to congratulate us and complimented Miss Shotwell on her game."

We headed back to the bar, and Sis rejoined her sister. I noticed Paltry boarding the bus back to the Prince Rupert; he was still wearing the bumblebee outfit.

Dick brought up tomorrow's matches and said it could be a grueling day, particularly if Miss Shotwell and I win the morning match. If we did, he offered to caddie for me. Little Rose was going to caddie for her sister in the morning, but she might be tired out if the match went to an additional eighteen holes. Dick offered to continue to caddie for me or Miss Shotwell. If I agreed, he offered to ask Finban Slattery or Alphie Jenkins to be my caddie. Both were available. Dick asked if I had any preference, and I told him that either would be fine since I had no experience with either one.

Dick said he would walk over to the small caddie house behind the first tee and see if either caddie would be available tomorrow. A short time later, he returned with Slattery. "Here's your man!"

I rose quickly from my chair to greet him.

Slattery said he was pleased to have a possible role to play in tomorrow's competition.

I asked if he would mind watching me hit a few balls to gain an impression of the distance I could hit the 5-wood and 6-iron. He and I walked over to the practice range and picked up a few balls. After hitting them with my driver, he wanted me to hit a few wedge shots. He nodded his approval and asked me to hit a few more balls with my driver, 5-wood, 3-iron, 6-iron, and 9-iron. We agreed I would use these clubs plus my wedge and putter tomorrow.

I returned to the veranda, and Dick was waiting for me. "After thinking about my plan again, we should talk to Sir Harold and Miss Shotwell before going any further with it." He had seen Sir Harold pick up Miss Shotwell and Rose and drive to Excelsior House.

I thought for a few seconds and agreed with him. We walked quickly to Excelsior House and knocked on the door.

A maid answered, and we said we wished to speak to Sir Harold and the ladies. She told us to wait while she informed Sir Harold of our presence.

Sir Harold came to the door almost immediately and welcomed us to come inside.

We explained our interest in having Dick caddie for Miss Shotwell if we won our morning match. We feared her little sister might be too tired after that match, and Dick said he would be delighted to caddie for Miss Shotwell if she was in the championship match.

Sir Harold thought for a minute and then said we should talk with the Shotwell girls. The ladies were enjoying cake and ice cream in the dining room. They seemed surprised to see us, and Sir Harold told them what we had a proposed for tomorrow's competition. Sir Harold explained that playing in the morning and the afternoon might be quite tiring for a caddie. "Therefore, Mr. Whistle would be willing to caddie in the afternoon for you, Forsythia."

Little Rose made a face, indicating she didn't agree with this proposal, but Forsythia said she could see the merit in this idea. Sir Harold suggested that Dick and I leave the room while they discussed the proposal. As we left, Miss Shotwell asked who the caddie might be for me.

Dick answered, "Finbarr Slattery has been a caddie at Gnomewood several times and knows the course well."

Dick and I went to the library for a cigarette and waited.

After a few minutes, Sir Harold came in to announce a decision had been made. Finbarr would caddie for me in the morning, and Rose would start with her sister. Should Forsythia and I win, a decision would then be made. If Rose felt too fatigued to continue as a caddie in the final match, Dick would carry the bag for Miss Shotwell in the afternoon. A final decision would be made tomorrow.

With that settled, we thanked the Shotwell girls for accepting our proposal and told them we felt confident about winning tomorrow. I felt relieved that the issue had been settled amicably. Sir Harold offered to have Leffingwell drive us back to the clubhouse to meet Slattery again and discuss the matches tomorrow.

Back at the clubhouse, I joined Slattery for a beer. We found two chairs on the veranda and were joined briefly by Bobby Clambourne, who was carrying the bag for Dr. Middlefield. Bobby said he and the doctor were about to head to the practice range. The doctor had not been pleased with his driving in the match against Quigley and Dedmon.

Slattery and I watched the doctor slam drive after drive to the right, to the left, and occasionally straight. Slattery said the doctor had a reputation as an erratic player, but when he was on his game, he was nearly unbeatable. I thought, *I hope Sis and I don't have to face him and Thistletoe in the final.*

I finished my beer and announced I was hungry. Dick was hungry too, but Slattery said he was going to wait until the doctor finished practice and join Clambourne back at their hotel.

Dick and I boarded the bus for the short trip back to the Prince Rupert. Dick suggested I look in the dining room for Ian Crankshaw. He and Tommy Sapwood had lost to Frogwell-Potts and Peebles and could offer some advice about competing against them.

Crankshaw was finishing his whiskey in the bar. In response to my interest in my match tomorrow, he said he would be glad to give me his impression of his opponents in their recently completed match. Dick and I found a table in the dining room, and we sat down to discuss Frogwell-Potts and Peebles.

Crankshaw said Peebles was in good form and didn't seem to have any flaws in his game except for maybe putts in the two-to-three-foot range. "Make him putt those if it's his turn. Frogwell-Potts and his lazy swing occasionally mishit wedge shots, leaving his partner with long chip shots or putts in the thirty-to-forty-foot range. And don't be put off by Frogwell-Potts eight-part backswing and two-part downswing that he manages to put together."

We all laughed and turned our attention to the menu. We all chose halibut chowder and a rather immature Chablis. Conversation centered around the upcoming Open.

Dick wondered if Bobby Locke would be successful in defending his title. Crankshaw said he thought Peter Thompson would regain the title he had won in 1956. Dick mentioned other golfers from Great Britain and Ireland who had made a favorable showing in last year's Ryder Cup, particularly Dai Rees and Christy O'Connor. Crankshaw agreed they should be considered, but he still thought Thompson was the man to beat.

After dinner, I decided to turn in early. My match was at nine o'clock, and I wanted to get to the course by seven thirty. I stopped at the registration desk to check on tomorrow's weather. A squall was predicted for later tonight, but it would be clearing by morning.

Back in my room, I finished some notes about today's play and took a shower.

CHAPTER 17

I must have slept through the early-morning squall because, on rising, I saw the sun easing its way through the remaining clouds. It looked like a good day to spend on the links. I donned my apparel for the day: dark blue slacks, a white golf shirt, and a yellow sweater. The aroma from the kitchen was drifting upstairs, and I was ready for breakfast. In the dining room, Dick was finishing breakfast and was about to leave for the links to chart flagstick positions. I said I would see him when it was near our tee time.

I sat alone but was soon joined by Geoff Cloverjoy, Fowler Thistletoe, and Patrick Quigly. As soon as he sat down, Cloverjoy asked how Miss Shotwell was playing. I said she was playing very well, and as her partner, she was carrying me along with her ability. Thistletoe said he was surprised to see she had shot a seventy-four in qualifying. I reminded him that her ability was well known among women golfers and that she was highly ranked in Great Britain. Thistletoe added that his partner, the doctor, had finished among the top five in the past three tournaments in which he played and, as his partner, they would be stiff competition. I didn't disagree with that warning.

Breakfast was served—scrambled eggs, ham, toast, and jam—to sustain us through the morning matches. While we were eating, Frogwell-Potts, who had joined us, asked me why Miss Shotwell and I had decided I should tee off on the first hole.

I answered, "If the match comes down to eighteen, she will tee off first. Today, she will tee off on the first hole. If I must tee off on eighteen, the hole should play downwind—and the second shot will be more important to us." I thought, *I must speak to Miss Shotwell as soon as I see her about who will lead off on the first hole.*

We devoured breakfast and finished tea. Several of us enjoyed a cigarette while Thistletoe spent a minute filling his pipe. I don't remember him lighting it. We finished our smoke, rose from the table, and walked out to the bus. I was beginning to sense a knot in my stomach. I glanced at my watch; it was 7:20.

The bus dropped us off at the clubhouse, and I saw my caddie, Finbarr Slattery, studying the green on the sixth hole. I could see the flagstick was on the lower left part of the green near the elephant grass. *Play safely to the center of the green,* I thought. He moved on to the green on thirteen, observing it briefly, and then to the sixteenth green. I proceeded to get my clubs from my locker, changed to my golf shoes, and headed to the practice range.

Thistletoe was walking to the range and looking over his shoulder for his partner.

I commented that the dentist was usually the last one on the range.

He told me he had been cautioned about this and looked forward to their upcoming match.

After stretching, I dumped out the practice balls from the sack and started practice. I proceeded from wedge to 9-iron and then 6-iron. I glanced back at the clubhouse and saw Dick, Miss Shotwell, and Rose walking to the range. Miss Shotwell was wearing knee-length shorts and a white sweater with blue trim. Rose was wearing denim blue bib overalls and a light blue shirt. Both had white visors.

As they arrived on the range, Miss Shotwell explained to Dick that she had been hitting short-iron shots behind Excelsior House. This was why she seemed late arriving at Gnomewood Links. She said, "Good morning, Mr. Nelson."

I thought it was time to tell her about my thoughts on changing our hitting order. I suggested she lead off on the first tee and continue in that order on the odd-numbered holes.

She listened for a minute and then said she looked forward to hearing her name introduced on the first tee. I felt relieved that she easily accepted this change from yesterday.

We commenced practice. Further down the range, our opponents, Frogwell-Potts and Peebles, were starting their warm-up. Both had a "languid beauty" to their swings, but Peebles accelerated into the ball more forcefully. Their opponents, Cloverjoy and Nippengay, had also started to practice. Both had short, compact swings. I thought the spectators would have an interesting experience comparing the different hitting styles.

When Sis and I began practicing with our drivers, she was at least twenty yards longer than my best effort, but we were both hitting the ball straight. Slattery cautioned me not to try to match her and to just stay with my game. I felt reasonably confident that if we made the final match, we could hold our own against the long-hitting Dr. Middlefield and shorter-hitting Fowler Thistletoe.

After practicing with our drivers, we decided to walk over to the practice putting green. We noticed the putts were rolling at about the same pace as yesterday. We both knew the greens would become faster as the breeze dried the surface. Our opponents joined us on the green, and we exchanged brief smiles of recognition.

At eight forty-five, I saw Sir Harold and Harley Bellows riding to the first tee. I took this as a signal to finish putting and suggested to Sis that we should head to the first tee. Dr. Middlefield and Thistletoe were playing in the match following us, and as we left the putting green, I heard the doctor tell Sis he hoped she would play well.

Waiting by the first tee were Miss Shotwell's parents, Dr. and Mrs. Reginald Shotwell. Dick had told me he was an orthopedic surgeon. He was a tall, distinguished-looking man with a firm handshake. He introduced his wife, Vera, an attractive, demure lady in a gray skirt, blue-gray sweater, and light blue headscarf. Mrs. Shotwell hugged her daughters and then commented on Sis wearing shorts.

Sis simply said it was the current style in America. I detected a hint of disapproval, but there was no further comment on her apparel.

Dr. Shotwell was interested in my clubs, "instruments," he called them, and he was particularly interested in my 5-wood. He commented on how new it appeared, and I said it was only a few months old. Slattery pulled the club from my bag and handed it to him. He waggled it a few times and commented on its excellent feel before handing it back to Slattery.

I asked Mrs. Shotwell if she played golf, and she replied, "Only on weekends, usually playing in mixed foursomes matches with the doctor. I have recently been playing with Rose during the week and can see that Rose is taking to the game."

I said, "Rose could learn a great deal about golf by caddying for her sister and watching her play."

Murmurs from the gallery—now comprised of some one hundred onlookers—indicated Sir Harold and Bellows were on the tee. The morning's competition was about to begin.

Sis and I walked onto the tee. We were followed by Frogwell-Potts and Peebles. Peebles wore a red sweater with a crocodile logo, a new fashion statement now worn by several golf professionals.

After polite applause died down, Bellows announced the start of the first match. "On the tee is Miss Forsythia Shotwell, recent winner of the Derby Ladies Amateur."

Cheers and applause followed this introduction. The gallery had been enhanced by the arrival of a group of young sportswriters from various parts of England.

Miss Shotwell tipped her visor to the gallery, teed up her ball, took two practice swings, and powered the ball some 240 yards down the fairway. Next on the tee was Winston Peebles. He was introduced as an up-and-coming young professional who would be one of the favorites in the Brighton Express tournament next month. Peebles took two whiplike practice swings and then blasted a drive some 280 yards down the left-center of the fairway.

As we walked down the fairway, Sis turned to me and said, "We will always be away and have the first shot to the green." She considered this an advantage in match play. I agreed with her. In my limited experience observing match play tournaments, a well-played shot to the green put added pressure on an opponent to match the shot.

Sis's tee shot left me with a 6-iron to the green. The flagstick was on the left, and I had a good angle to the flag. My 6-iron landed short of the flag and ran some six feet farther.

Frogwell-Potts was on the left side of the fairway and had to thread the needle to the hole or play away from the flag. He struck a short iron that ended up some twenty feet from the cup. Peebles addressed the twenty-footer and stroked it, just missing the left edge.

Sis stroked the six-footer, and it touched the right edge of the cup—but it failed to drop. The remaining putts were conceded.

I teed off first on the second hole, a 385-yard par-4. I took two practice swings to loosen up and then smacked a drive of some 220 yards down the right-center of the fairway. Frogwell-Potts followed with a drive of about the same length. Our partners hit the green with their second shots, leaving putts in the twelve-to-fifteen-foot range. Potts and I missed the birdie putts, and the short remaining putts were conceded.

We came to the third hole, a 503-yard par-5 dogleg left. Sis hit a drive that faded slightly, landing at the edge of the beets. Peebles then drove some twenty yards farther—into the beets. I had a shot to the green from the short rough. I thought it was an ideal shot for my 5-wood. Slattery had already pulled the club. After several practice swings, I hit a solid shot to the fairway, leaving Sis with a shot of about seventy yards to the green.

Frogwell-Potts had a more difficult shot. He had to drop from the beets into rough that was several inches high. He elected to hit a 3-wood and smothered the shot, advancing the ball maybe one hundred yards or so. This left Peebles with what I assumed would be a midiron to the green, but he chose to hit an 8-iron or a 9-iron. Hitting into a breeze, the shot came up short of the green. The next shot was Sis's, and she stroked a wedge to about five feet from the flag. Frogwell-Potts was now hitting their fourth shot, and he hit a short-iron to about eight feet from the cup. On the green, Peebles struck a putt for par that just missed, running two feet past the hole. I now had a five-foot birdie putt that I left a few inches short. Our par putt was conceded. We were now 1-up.

The short fourth hole, a par-3, was halved, as was the fifth hole, a par-4. This hole was also halved. Throughout the tournament, hole 6 had presented a challenge to all the teams. The dogleg left bent about where the elephant grass was located in the left rough. A straight drive of more than 250 yards risked landing through the fairway and in the carrots. I wasn't sure I could hit a controlled draw around the dogleg. Slattery and I thought I should aim at the left-center of the fairway and play a slight fade. As in the previous round, I felt confident in playing this shot. I mentioned this plan to Sis, and she agreed. I struck a good drive that faded a bit too much and landed on the edge of the right rough some 210 yards away.

Frogwell-Potts was now on the tee. I thought he might have an advantage because he tended to draw or hook his drives. If he could draw the ball around the dogleg, he would leave his partner with a short iron to the green. On the tee, he and Peebles conferred. I saw Peebles pointing to the right side of the fairway. Apparently, they were following my strategy and avoiding any chance of hooking the ball into the elephant grass. In addressing the ball, I noted Frogwell-Potts fingering the grip to open the clubface. This would eliminate a tendency to hook the ball into the elephant grass. He then drove the ball down the fairway some 240 yards before it began to fade too much, landing beyond the carrots and in deep rough.

We walked to our respective drives. Peebles found their ball and could only blast out of the rough with a wedge, leaving his partner some thirty yards short of the green. Next to hit was Sis. She hit a 6-iron to about fifteen feet from the flagstick. Frogwell-Potts was up next. He played a soft wedge to the green that stopped about eight feet from the cup. I now had a left-to-right birdie putt of fifteen feet. I stroked what I thought was a good putt, but it broke just before the hole on the low side. Peebles observed how my putt broke and stroked a putt that rolled into the cup, saving par. We remained 1-up.

The seventh hole was halved with bogies as both drives landed in the celery, and the second shots missed the green, leaving difficult chip shots and putts.

The par-3 eighth hole was halved, and it was on to the ninth hole, a 525-yard par-5. Sis hammered a 240-yard drive that the breeze carried into the eggplants. Peebles was next up, and he drove into one of the fairway bunkers on the left.

Walking to Sis's drive, I saw I would have an easier shot at the green. The rough around the drop zone stake was relatively short, and my 5-wood was handed to me by Slattery. I hit a solid shot that landed about thirty yards short of the green.

Frogwell-Potts stepped into the bunker with a wood in his hand, probably his 3-wood. I couldn't tell how close to the lip of the bunker he was, but I would not have chosen that club. He swung, and the ball clipped the edge of the bunker, landing some one hundred yards short of the green. Peebles then played a short iron to about twenty feet from the flag. Sis then stroked a short wedge shot to about five feet from the cup.

On the green, Frogwell-Potts had a twenty-footer that he ran by several feet. I had a five-footer for a birdie that I just missed, the ball running about a foot beyond the hole. This short putt was conceded. Peebles walked back and forth, surveying their three-footer and expecting us to concede their putt.

Sis murmured to me not to concede. I shook my head.

Peebles finally stood over their putt for a few seconds and then sank it. Thus, we halved the hole and remained 1-up.

We paused at the refreshment area between the green on nine and the tee area on ten. I thought Frogwell-Potts showed great sportsmanship when he directed little Rose to Danish rolls. She quickly consumed one before starting a second. Sis pretended to have wanted the second roll but settled on a cheese sandwich and a bottle of apple juice. I had a sausage sandwich and a lemonade. Our opponents selected sausage and beer. We rested for about ten minutes before starting the back nine.

Both teams parred the tenth hole and moved on to the 212-yard par-3 eleventh hole. The hole played into a breeze, and Sis selected a 3-iron for her tee shot. She started the shot over the edge of the lettuce and let the ball draw back toward the green. The ball landed at the base of the green.

Peebles also hit a 3-iron that was low and stayed below the wind. It appeared headed for the flag, but at the last second, it hooked and landed on the left side of the green, rolling into a bunker. Peebles and Frogwell-Potts walked to the bunker, and Peebles pointed to a spot on the green where Frogwell-Potts's shot should land. Frogwell-Potts took several practice swings and then blasted the ball out well beyond where Peebles had pointed. This left a putt of about twenty feet.

My putt from the base of the green was about thirty feet from the flag. Sis pointed out the right-to-left break and said I should aim an inch outside the right edge of the hole. I could see the line and wanted to hit a firm putt that would die at the hole. After several practice strokes, I rapped a putt that was online, but it came up several inches short. This was conceded.

Peebles had a twenty-footer to save par. He surveyed the putt from all angles, took his stance, and stroked it into the cup. The spectators applauded this effort. We remained 1-up.

The twelfth hole was a par-4 of 365 yards. Both drives were down the middle, but Frogwell-Potts outdrove me by twenty yards. Our partners hit iron shots to the green that resulted in putts of no more than five feet. Neither sportswriter could sink his birdie putt.

Hole 13 was a 145-yard par-3, flanked by an onion patch on the left and dense rough on the right. Behind the green was a deep bunker, which players knew to avoid at this point in the tournament. Peebles and Sis hit tee shots that landed just short of the green. Frogwell-Potts was first to play. He used a putter that came up about two feet short. I elected to chip with an 8-iron and ran the chip about two feet beyond the cup. Both teams decided to concede these short putts.

The fourteenth hole was a 517-yard par-5 dogleg left that played into the wind. An extensive growth of mustard flanked the right side of the fairway, and three pot bunkers guarded the left side where the fairway began to bend. Slattery advised me to hit a draw if I could. The breeze would hold up the ball just short of the bunkers. I took several practice swings, closed my stance slightly, and hit what I thought was an excellent drive. It did draw slightly and landed just short of the first bunker.

Our opponents now stood on the tee. Frogwell-Potts was a longer driver than me, and he decided to play along the right side of the fairway and avoid the bunkers. After several vigorous practice swings, he hammered a long drive that the breeze wafted into the mustard.

We walked to our respective tee shots. Sis had a perfect lie in the fairway, but it was nearly three hundred yards from the green. Undaunted by the distance, she uncorked a 3-wood close to 240 yards, leaving me with an easy 6-iron to the green.

Our opponents seemed to be taking a long time to find their ball. Finally, they found it and dropped in in the area by the green-and-white stake. The rough there appeared to be about three inches high. Peebles selected a 3-wood for his shot. I thought a midiron would be a safer play, but he swung—and the ball clipped the top of the mustard and landed short of where Sis's 3-wood had landed.

Frogwell-Potts was away, and he fired a 6-iron that the breeze drifted to the right side of the green some forty feet from the flagstick.

I hit an easy 6-iron, aiming at the left-center of the green, and the ball landed and stopped about twelve feet from the cup. Peebles now had a forty-foot putt that he stroked some three feet short of the cup. Sis had a twelve-foot putt for a birdie, but she missed the putt. The ball rolled over the left edge of the hole and stopped a foot away.

Frogwell-Potts had to sink the three-footer for par. We weren't about to concede it. He looked at it for a minute and then addressed the putt. Several seconds passed before he drew the putter head back and tapped a putt that stopped a foot from the cup. Our short putt was conceded, and we were now 2-up.

The short fifteenth hole was halved with par.

The par-4 sixteenth hole was playing downwind. The main dangers were a large, deep bunker in the potato patch along the right side of the fairway and a deep bunker behind the green. I managed to hit my drive some 230 yards down the middle. Frogwell cranked out a drive of some 250 yards also down the middle. Our partners' iron shots landed on the green. I had a twenty-foot putt that ran by the cup, leaving a two-footer for par. Frogwell had a ten-footer that stopped inches from the cup. We conceded this putt. Sis paused briefly, expecting the two-footer to be conceded, but our opponents remained silent. There was a slight left-to-right break in the putt, and we both decided she should aim just inside the left lip. Out opponents were watching intently as she lined up the putt, hoping, I think, she would miss it. She sank it, and the match was now dormie.

The seventeenth hole was 440 yards into the stiffening breeze. The left side of the fairway was flanked by a pot bunker followed by a heavy growth of spinach. Slattery advised Sis to aim slightly left and let the breeze carry the ball to the right-center of the fairway. As soon as she hit her drive, I could see it was going to drift into the spinach.

Peebles stepped to the tee and said with a smile that we were giving them a break. He then smacked a drive some 260 yards down the left-center of the fairway—just where Sis had intended to hit her drive.

We walked to where her drive had landed, and I lifted it from the spinach and dropped it in grass that was about three inches high. Peebles walked over to observe the drop. Slattery pulled my 5-wood and told me to just make good contact; Sis agreed that it was the right choice. The ball was partially sitting up, and I felt confident I could hit it at least two hundred yards. I took several practice swings before addressing the ball. I then smacked a solid shot that landed about twenty yards from the green. We had a definite chance at par.

Frogwell-Potts addressed his shot. He struck a midiron that appeared to be online with the flagstick, but it rose in the breeze and faded into a bunker guarding the green on the right.

At that point, it was Miss Shotwell's twenty-yard pitch shot versus Peebles's bunker shot to decide the hole and possibly the match. She took several practice swings, and then used her wedge to loft a shot that stopped about three feet from the flag. She quickly walked to her ball and marked it.

Peebles entered the bunker, waggled his feet in the sand, and took several practice swings. He then blasted the ball out to about two feet from the cup.

I had to make the three-footer to save par and the match. I felt a bit nervous as I lined up the putt.

Sis and Slattery agreed it was straight with no break. Sis looked at me and said, "Don't leave it short!"

I took my stance and could see a straight line to the cup. I gripped and regripped my putter, and then I drew it back and swung through the ball. The sound of the ball hitting the back of the cup was partially drowned out by the applause from the gallery. We won two and one.

Sis picked up our opponents' ball marker and handed it to Frogwell-Potts. Handshakes followed along with congratulatory words. I took Sis's golf bag from Rose and told her she had done an admirable job for her sister.

When I also thanked Finbarr Slattery for his efforts as a caddie, he replied. "With that lady as your partner, I didn't feel much need to offer advice."

Back in the clubhouse, there were tea and sandwiches. Sis and little Rose joined her parents and Sir Harold to return to Excelsior House. In departing, Sis said she would meet me on the practice range at one thirty.

Dick and I found a table and sat down. Dick saw the two Scotsmen who had been following the matches and asked if I minded if they joined us. I told him I would welcome their comments on my match. Crankshaw said it was a pleasure watching Miss Shotwell and hoped she would play later this year in the Dundee Ladies Match Play Tournament.

Our conversation ended when the players and spectators from the other semifinal match entered the clubhouse. The doctor and Thistletoe headed for the bar, ordered a beer, and looked at the lunch table. Judging from their ebullient attitude, I assumed they had won. The Scotsmen had followed the match intermittently and said the match had been close.

John B. Nanninga

Dick had watched the last hole where the doctor's 3-wood had landed just short of the green, leading to a birdie and 1-up victory.

The clubhouse was beginning to fill up, and the air was filled with smoke from cigarettes and an immature cigar. I said I wanted to go out on the veranda and sink into one of the wicker chairs. Dick thought this was an excellent idea, and we located two chairs in which to relax and gaze out on the eighteenth hole.

I noted the flag was now fluttering, indicating the breeze was increasing. I said, "This should help my driving distance downwind, particularly on eighteen."

Dick replied, "The doctor and Thistletoe will usually outdrive you and Miss Shotwell, but don't be intimidated. You both stood up to the competition in your match this morning."

I said, "I will keep my 3-iron in my bag; it has a lower flight and will be more useful in hitting into the wind."

154

CHAPTER 18

I dozed off for maybe thirty minutes, and Dick awakened me and said Miss Shotwell was arriving at the clubhouse. I saw Slattery plodding toward the practice range with my clubs. Dick said he would meet Miss Shotwell and her sister in the clubhouse, assuming he would caddie for her this afternoon. I walked to the range, greeted Slattery, and started to warm up. Thistletoe had also arrived at the range and started to practice, but there was no sign of his partner.

When Dick and Miss Shotwell arrived on the range, she had changed to red shorts and a white sweater with red polka dots.

I walked over to where she had started to warm up and said, "If we play as we did this morning, we should give Fowler Thistletoe and the doctor a tough match."

She replied in a stern voice, "I think we can handle them."

I admired her confidence. I resumed practice, concentrating on my driver.

Slattery was watching and observed that I tended to open the face of my driver at the top of my backswing. That explained why I was fading the ball on some holes and even hitting the occasional slice. It was good advice, and I began to draw the ball on my drives.

A roar from an automobile in the parking lot signaled the arrival of Dr. Middlefield and his wife. From the caddie house, Bobby Clambourne emerged with the doctor's clubs.

I said to Thistletoe, "There's your partner." I handed my driver to Slattery, and we headed to the practice putting green. I glanced back to where Sis was practicing; she was banging out drives some 240 yards. This was reassuring.

She soon joined me on the putting green. We putted for about ten minutes before we were joined by Thistletoe and the doctor. I glanced at their putting strokes to see if I could detect any flaws. The doctor was missing his putts long, and I wondered if he had been taking his pep pills.

It was 1:55, and we were to tee off at 2:00. We, along with our opponents, walked to the first tee. I estimated there was a crowd of maybe a hundred spectators waiting to follow the final match.

Harley Bellows saw us and promptly announced, "The championship match will be played by Miss Forsythia Shotwell and her partner, Mr. John Nelson, versus Dr. Carrington Middlefield, who was on last year's winning team, and Mr. Fowler Thistletoe. Miss Shotwell has the honors."

Enthusiastic applause greeted us.

Sis then blasted a drive of close to 250 yards down the right-center of the fairway. The doctor followed with a drive of some 280 yards left-center in the fairway.

I had a good lie in the fairway and smacked a 6-iron to the green. Thistletoe had a short iron to the green that he hit to about twenty feet from the flagstick. Sis and the doctor just missed birdie putts, leaving short putts that were conceded.

The second hole was also halved with par, and it was on to the third hole, a par-5. Again, Dr. Middlefield outdrove Sis by some thirty yards. I was next to play from the fairway, and I hit my 5-wood about one hundred yards short of the green. Thistletoe struck a 3-wood to about twenty yards short of the green. Sissy then struck a wedge to about ten feet from the flagstick. The doctor then chipped to about two feet from the flag. I missed my birdie putt, and Thistletoe sank the two-footer. They were now 1-up.

The fourth hole, a par-3, was halved, as was the par-4 fifth hole. Moving on to the difficult sixth hole, Thistletoe was on the tee. At this point in the tournament, both teams were quite aware of the elephant grass on the left and the dogleg that bent to the left. Thistletoe appeared to have overcompensated by aiming his drive to the right, hoping to land in the right fairway or the carrots. He struck a long slice that landed beyond the carrots, in the deep rough. I struck a drive that landed short of the elephant grass, giving Sissy a relative straight shot to the green.

We spent several minutes looking for Thistletoe's drive before finding it nestled in the rough. The doctor stooped down to identify the ball before stepping back and taking several vigorous practice swings with an 8-iron. He then blasted the ball, grass, and turf onto the fairway.

Sissy was now away. She hit a 6-iron to the green. Thistletoe was next to hit and had a chance to redeem himself, but he drilled a 6-iron that landed and rolled to the back of the green. The doctor had the next shot. He had a downhill putt for par that he stroked some four feet beyond the cup. I had a fifteen-foot putt for birdie that I rolled over the right edge, stopping about a foot beyond the cup. This was conceded, and our par gave us the hole and evened the match.

Holes 7 and 8 were halved, and we moved on to the ninth hole, a par-5. Sissy was on the tee. She struck a good tee shot that landed near the edge of a fairway pot bunker on the left. The doctor then stepped up and blasted a long drive that hooked into the second fairway pot bunker on the left. I found I had a good lie in the short rough at the edge of the fairway and smacked a 5-wood that landed about eighty yards short of the green.

From the bunker, Thistletoe had no choice but to use a short iron to escape. He successfully blasted out, leaving the doctor with a 3-iron to the green. He hammered a shot that landed at the base of the green and rolled to about ten feet from the flag. Sissy then played our third shot with a wedge to about five feet from the flag, Thistletoe had a putt for birdie that missed by several inches and stopped a foot from the cup. I had an excellent chance to birdie the hole and sank the five-footer. We were now 1-up.

We faced the back nine with a 1-up lead. There was a brief noise from the yellow-breasted ratchets after someone in the gallery disturbed them. Their noise gradually subsided.

At the refreshment cart, Sis and I had a cookie and lemonade. Sis took a cookie for little Rose, who had been following the match and would be joined by her parents on fourteen. I took a beer for Slattery. The doctor and Thistletoe chose cheese sandwiches and ginger ale. I heard the doctor say to Clambourne that he hoped the damn birds would remain quiet when we teed off. After saying that, he opened a small metal tube and removed a pill that he took with the ginger ale. By now, the birds had quieted down. We were ready to start play.

Facing hole 10, Thistletoe and I hit drives down the middle. Our partners hit short-iron shots that found the green, and both sides two-putted for par.

We now faced the difficult par-3 eleventh hole. I sensed the breeze had increased, and on the tee, Miss Shotwell noticed this too. She elected to hit a 3-iron, realizing her shot might come up short, but his would leave me with an uphill chip shot. She struck a shot that started at the green, but it drifted into the edge of the lettuce.

The doctor saw this and hammered a 3-iron that landed on the back edge of the green and rolled into a bunker.

Walking to our ball, I saw I would have a drop in relatively short rough. I then played a wedge to no more than five feet from the cup.

Thistletoe, in the bunker, blasted out to the edge of the green. The doctor was left with a twenty-five-foot putt that he rolled several feet beyond the hole.

Sissy had a five-foot putt to win the hole. She rolled it in, and we won the hole. I complimented her on the putt, and she replied with a smile, "It was easy." We were now 2-up.

We halved the twelfth and thirteenth holes and moved on to the

517-yard fourteenth. This hole was a challenge for me because I was the shortest driver.

On the tee, Sissy said, "Swing easy and just keep it in the fairway."

I realized I couldn't reach the bunkers on the left or where the mustard on the right met the pea patch along the neighboring fifteenth fairway. Consequently, I took a smooth, easy swing and propelled a drive down the left side of the fairway.

Thistletoe stepped to the tee and hammered a draw that landed in a bunker.

Sissy was next to play and hit a 3-wood that landed in the fairway, leaving me with a wedge to the green.

When the doctor approached their ball in the bunker, he found it partially buried. He had initially taken a 3-wood for his next shot, but Clambourne handed him a midiron. After several practice swings, he blasted out to about where Sissy's shot had landed.

I couldn't help but admire his ability, and the gallery gave their applause for his escape from the bunker.

At this point, Thistletoe and I would have short-iron shots to the green. I was away, and I struck a firm wedge that stopped about seven feet from the flag. The pressure was now on Thistletoe to match my shot. He took several practice swings and then swung and stabbed the turf behind the ball, sending a large divot and the ball down the fairway about twenty yards short of the green. The doctor now had a long chip to the green. He took an 8-iron and played a running chip that stopped about two and a half feet from the cup.

On the green, Sissy had the seven-footer for birdie. She stroked a good putt that stopped several inches short. She kicked her putter in disgust as she marked the ball.

The doctor conceded the par putt, and our opponents waited to see if we would concede their par putt.

Sissy finally said, "I think you should putt it."

Thistletoe and the doctor stared at us for a few seconds before Thistletoe addressed the putt. Sissy and I stepped to the back of the green, leaving the stage to Thistletoe. He and the doctor looked at the putt again before the doctor said, "Sink it." Applause from the gallery told us he made it. We remained 2-up.

The short fifteenth hole was halved with par. Next up was sixteen, a 400-yard par-4, with a growth of potatoes along the right side of the fairway and a large bunker within it. Behind the green, there was also a deep bunker. I was on the tee, and after several practice swings, I smacked a drive of some 230 yards along the left side of the fairway.

Thistletoe uncorked a drive of some 250 yards. Our partners hit the green with their shots, and two putts later, we moved on to the seventeenth. The match was now dormie.

Seventeen was a 440-yard par-4 playing into the wind. A large growth of spinach was located along the right side of the fairway. Sis and I conferred briefly before I saw her aim along the left fairway and slam a drive of some 240 yards.

The doctor followed by belting a drive some 270 yards down the middle.

I found I would have a shot of about two hundred yards to the green, which was ideal for my 5-wood. The doctor and Thistletoe walked to where I was standing. They stood aside as I was ready to hit, but they were still in my field of vision. I hit what I thought was an excellent shot, but the ball hung up in the breeze and fell about ten yards short of the green.

The next shot was Thistletoe's. He hit a 6-iron that landed on the green and rolled to about six feet from the flag. Sissy then struck a chip shot that landed about five feet from the flag. I would have a putt for par, and the doctor would have a putt for birdie.

On the green, the doctor quickly surveyed the putts and said I was away. Sis, Slattery, and I determined my putt broke about on inch outside the left lip. As soon as I struck it, I thought I had made it—but the ball stopped a few inches short. The doctor told me to pick it up. I had a sick feeling I had lost the hole. The doctor lined up his six-footer and sank it. We were now only 1-up and starting hole 18.

Eighteen was a 565-yard par-5 playing downwind. Thistletoe was on the tee. He took several robust practice swings before launching a wild drive that hooked beyond the tomatoes and landed in deep rough. "Damn it!" He wheeled and threw his driver into the sea.

Someone clapped. Two young boys who had been following the match and were probably looking for lost golf balls, ran to the water's edge, waded into the surf, and looked for the driver.

Slattery handed me my driver and told me to try not to kill it. I took two leisurely practice swings and stroked a drive the wind carried some 240 yards down the middle.

Thistletoe and the doctor began a search for the errant tee shot. After several minutes, they found the ball in the deep rough. Clambourne handed the doctor an iron, and after several explosive practice swings, the doctor blasted the ball out of the rough and into a bunker on the opposite side of the fairway.

Sissy was now away. She struck a 3-wood some 220 yards down the fairway, leaving me with a short-iron to the green.

From the bunker, Thistletoe blasted out fifty yards down the fairway. Following this, the doctor struck a 6-iron to the green, the ball rolling to about twenty feet from the flagstick. That was their fourth shot. It was up to me to hit the green with my 8-iron. I took several nervous practice swings and then struck a shot that landed about twelve feet from the flagstick. I sensed we would win even if Thistletoe sank the twenty-footer. And he did—and then he bowed to an applauding gallery. Sissy lined up the twelve-foot birdie putt and sank it. We won 2-up!

There were cheers and applause from the gallery.

I shook Slattery's hand and then our opponents' hands.

The doctor gave Miss Shotwell a hug and said, "You and the Yank were too good today."

I gave Sissy a hug and told her how fortunate I was to have had her as a partner.

Spectators were moving onto the green to congratulate us, and Dick quickly took Miss Shotwell to where the BBC had a microphone and camera.

The interviewer was Charles Thinwood, brother of one of the golf writers playing in the tournament. His questions were what I would have asked: "How did it feel to compete against men? Did you feel any hostility during the tournament? Will you compete again in any other tournaments with men?"

I don't recall her exact answers, but I thought she handled the interview very adeptly.

The two boys who had fished Thistletoe's driver from the water presented it to him. He thanked them, reached into his pocket for a coin for each of them, and said he would use it again.

While walking to the clubhouse, several young sportswriters, who couldn't get close enough to Miss Shotwell to question her, asked me if I knew her instructor. I said I assumed it was her father, but I didn't know more about her golf experience. One asked, "Does she have a boyfriend?" Again, I couldn't answer. Finally, one of the young men congratulated me on my play. He thought Americans playing in the British Islands didn't understand links golf. Their shots were too high and bounced off the greens—or their drives ran into bunkers that they should have avoided. I said I was fortunate to have had Miss Shotwell as a partner and Dick Whistle as a friend and coach. Plus, my caddie, Finbarr Slattery, was valuable in knowing Gnomewood Links.

The young men drifted over to where Miss Shotwell was finishing her interview with the BBC, hoping to get her to answer a few of their questions.

Dr. Middlefield emerged from the clubhouse, drink in hand, and motioned me over to where Sir Harold was talking with a man and a tall, stately woman. Sir Harold greeted me and introduced me to Joyce Wethered (Lady Heathcoat-Amory) and her husband. He said Miss Wethered was one of the outstanding women golfers of the previous generation, and in his opinion, no other lady golfer in Great Britain compared with her. He added that we had just witnessed a young lady who may very well approach her in ability and accomplishments.

A few older sportswriters moved over to this impromptu gathering. They recognized Miss Wethered and were eager to hear her impression of Miss Shotwell.

Miss Wethered said she had watched her play the back nine today and had observed her competing in previous tournaments. She was quite impressed with her ability and composure. She then asked me my impression of her.

I said, "As a member of the winning team, she was invaluable in providing advice and bolstering my confidence. Having observed golf in the States, I feel she can compete in our Women's Amateur and do quite well—even in our Women's National Open."

Miss Wethered agreed and was sure Miss Shotwell would rise to the top in women's golf in the British Isles.

Dick walked over to where Sir Harold's group was gathered and called me aside. He said he and I and the Shotwells were invited to Excelsior House for dinner, and the Heathcoat-Amorys would be there. Dick recalled how he had interviewed Joyce Wethered some years ago after an exhibition match and said how gracious she was in granting time to a young reporter.

I walked back to the clubhouse and looked for Finbarr. Someone said they had seen him sitting by the caddie house with Bobby Clambourne and Alphie Judson. I wanted to thank him again for his efforts in the match. The three were about to leave for the Foggy Shores and its pub, the Storm Petrel, and they invited me to join them later this evening if I were free.

I told them that I hoped they would be on their feet when I got there. That brought a laugh from all three. I folded a twenty-pound note and slipped it Finbarr's shirt pocket. He thanked me and said he hoped to see me next year.

I rejoined a group of reporters who were still interviewing Miss Shotwell. Sir Harold walked over and asked players and friends to come inside the clubhouse. He said emphatically that the press was not allowed inside and asked those already inside to please leave. "Miss Shotwell and Mr. Nelson need time to relax and savor their victory."

Once inside, Miss Shotwell was offered a glass of champagne, which she graciously accepted. I asked for a gin and tonic, and it was quickly served. Little Rosie was now in the group, having a glass of ginger ale and taking in all the fuss and celebration. Dr. and Mrs. Shotwell were escorted into the clubhouse and interviewed. Outside the clubhouse, the jeep pulled up, and the Heathcoat-Amorys departed for Excelsior House.

Dr. Middlefield entered the clubhouse after chatting with the press corps by the practice green. Someone had produced a putter, and he was giving an impromptu demonstration of putting technique. He saw Dick and said how much he had enjoyed being his partner last year.

Dick returned the compliment by saying anyone partnered with the doctor had an excellent chance of winning. "Look how close you and Fowler came to winning today."

The doctor acknowledged how he and his sportswriter partners had been successful at Gnomewood in previous years.

Sir Harold moved behind the bar, tapped on a glass, and announced that those inside the clubhouse were invited to Excelsior House for dinner at seven o'clock. Dr. and Mrs. Shotwell had already been taken in the jeep to Excelsior House, but Forsythia and Rose boarded the bus along with the rest of us. The bus dropped them off at Excelsior House before taking us to the Prince Rupert.

Before I boarded the bus, I deposited ten pounds in a caddie bag that would be distributed by Sir Harold to the caddies who had worked in the tournament.

CHAPTER 19

Back at the Prince Rupert, I took a quick shower and put on a dark blue blazer, white dress shirt, tie, and gray plus fours with stockings with a blue-and-red pattern. After donning my dinner attire, I ventured down to the lobby. Fowler Thistletoe was also wearing a blazer, shirt, tie, and gray plus fours, and Dick was wearing a dark gray suit. We viewed each other and decided we would pass inspection from Sir Harold.

Within a few minutes, the jeep arrived, and the three of us rode to Excelsior House. Sir Harold introduced us to his guests as outstanding sportswriters and enthusiastic golfers. He mentioned that I was on the winning team with Miss Shotwell. We were escorted to the library, where the Shotwells were conversing with Lady Heathcoat-Amory, and Sir Harold motioned to me to follow him. We walked into his study, and he asked if I wished to make a long-distance call to my wife.

I replied, "I certainly do—and I was planning to do so from my hotel."

He picked up a phone, handed it to me, pushed a green button, and told me to wait a minute. Within a few seconds, a voice came on requesting a number. I said I was calling the States and gave my home number. Another voice came on and asked me to please standby. At this point, Sir Harold left the room.

Within two minutes, Barbara's voice came on and asked, "Is that you, John?"

I answered, "Yes, I'm calling to let you know that John Nelson was on the winning team."

She said she was thrilled to hear the news and looked forward to hearing all the details when I returned.

We chatted for a few more minutes before she asked who was paying for the call.

166

I laughed and said, "It's on the house. I will tell you more when I return."

We expressed our love, and then I said I would see her soon and ended the call.

I walked back to the library. Champagne was being served, and Sir Harold asked if the phone connection was satisfactory.

I said, "It was, and I appreciate the opportunity to make the call."

The Shotwells walked over to where Sir Harold and I were standing and expressed their appreciation for my partnership with their daughter.

I glanced at Sir Harold and said, "It was Sir Harold's doing, and I was fortunate to have such a talented partner. I had never played foursomes, and Forsythia guided me along. I knew we made the right decision to have her tee off in today's matches."

Her father replied, "She is a winner—no matter the order in which you play."

Dinner was served, and I was seated next to the former Miss Wethered. As the salad was being served, I asked her who among the American women golfers had impressed her the most.

She answered, "In the era in which I competed, Glenna Collett (Vare) was outstanding. She had a powerful game, and I was fortunate to have defeated her in our amateur championship. After that, there was Babe Didrikson. She won our amateur championship before she became a professional. She was the longest hitter I witnessed among women players."

I reminded her that Bobby Jones had complimented her on her swing and all-around game, and then I asked if she had ever seen Mr. Jones play. She smiled and reminded me that her brother Roger, an outstanding golfer in his own right, had lost to Jones in the initial Walker Cup singles matches in 1922, and she had watched Jones defeat her brother during the Walker Cup matches in 1930. Later that year, he defeated him again in the finals of the Amateur at St. Andrews.

I felt somewhat embarrassed at my ignorance of this history, replying, "I suspect your brother had seen enough of Mr. Jones."

Miss Wethered said today's professional women's ranks offered an avenue to compete and win prize money. She had no interest in playing professionally, but she admired the American professionals Patty Berg, Louise Suggs, and Betsy Rawls. To her, amateur golf had become more expensive, and it required family financial backing to compete successfully in amateur tournaments. Currently, tennis seems to attract more athletically inclined girls. She added that Miss Shotwell should be a role model for girls taking up golf as a sport.

Dinner was then served. The first course, a vegetable salad made from products grown on Gnomewood Links, was followed by a seafood stew accompanied by champagne. Conversation turned to the economic recovery of Europe and Great Britain. We all agreed that the improved financial situation around the world should lead to more participation in golf. Public golf courses had been renovated, leading to more opportunities to play golf.

Speaking of finances, I inquired if there was talk of increasing the purse for the Open. American professionals had said the trip to compete in the Open cost them money, above what prize money would have covered. That was supposedly why Sam Snead didn't return to defend his Open title in 1946.

Sir Harold responded that there wasn't enough sponsorship money to substantially increase the prize money. Bobby Locke, from South Africa, and Peter Thompson, from Australia, most likely had financial backing from golf equipment manufacturers, clothing companies, and perhaps subsidies from various golf clubs and societies. Exhibitions also added to their incomes. Finally, gate receipts were a main source of prize money, and while Ben Hogan drew large crowds at Carnoustie, there was less interest in the Open if an Englishman or Scot wasn't favored to win. In the future, fees from media, radio, and television should increase the amounts of prize money.

During a lull in conversation, Dr. Shotwell asked about my interest in golf. I said I had played on my college golf team and wrote a weekly column about the team in the school newspaper during the golf season. In journalism school, I didn't have much time to play golf, but I had reported on golf, tennis, and baseball. After graduation, my first job was with an upstate New York newspaper, but that only lasted a year before I entered the army as a war correspondent, reporting on the Eighth Air Force.

"After the war, I was fortunate to return to my previous employer, where I covered baseball, ice hockey, and local golf tournaments. My big break came in golf reporting when I approached our sports editor about covering the Ryder Cup, which was being played in Ganton, in 1949. The newspaper was doing reasonably well financially, and I thought it could afford to send a sportswriter who could tolerate British cooking and budget hotels. I emphasized the growing popularity of golf since the war—and that Ben Hogan was the nonplaying captain of the American team. Hogan's name was well known to any reader of the sports pages—even if they had only a passing interest in golf.

"The editor had brought my proposal to the owner of the paper, and he happened to be an avid golfer and member at two private clubs. After about a week, I received the good news that my trip had been approved. However, it came with a warning: I should be 'as frugal as possible' and 'avoid staying in London except when arriving and departing.'

"When I arrived in London, I was able to book a reservation at Scarborough, near Ganton, at a rather dilapidated hotel that had housed American servicemen. On arriving in Scarborough, I found the room had a makeshift shower and a small desk. I was interested in what the local newspaper was reporting on the Ryder Cup. To my surprise, the US captain, Ben Hogan, had objected to what he perceived to be the deep grooves on the irons of some members of the British team. The issue was referred to the Royal & Ancient, which finally decided to have a local professional file down the grooves on the questionable irons. One of the members of the R&A who ruled on the matter was Bernard Darwin, an outstanding golf writer and grandson of Charles Darwin. The matches began favorably for the Great Britain and Ireland team, and they won three out of four foursomes matches. However, the tide turned the next day when the American team won six out of eight singles matches.

"I thoroughly enjoyed reporting this event, and my account of the Ryder Cup in the local paper was picked up by a New York City sports editor. He subsequently contacted me about the possibility of working for his paper. Two weeks later, we met during a Dodgers baseball game. Following the game, he offered me a job. I told him I would talk with my wife about this opportunity, but I would welcome the opportunity to cover sports in New York—as well as other parts of the country where New York teams competed.

"When I returned home, I spoke with Barbara about the job offer. She was enthusiastic about my offer and living in New York. I accepted. I notified the local newspaper, which had given me my first job, and thanked my editor and the owner for the start they had provided to my career. In parting, the editor said he recognized my ability to tell a story and make it interesting, and he knew I would be successful in the Big City."

Sir Harold had been listening to this rather one-sided conversation with Dr. Shotwell and asked me what my preferred sport was to cover. I answered it was a toss-up between golf and baseball. He expressed an interest in my reporting on certain American golf tournaments, namely the Masters, the United States Open, and the PGA championship.

He would like my reports to appear in one of his newspapers and, in a condensed version, in his publication, *Fin, Feather & Fairways*. I was flattered, and I said I would consider it an honor to submit my accounts of these tournaments to his publications. We shook hands to seal the agreement.

I didn't have much time to talk with Forsythia and Rosie because I was sitting farther down the table, but when I rose to leave, I walked over to where Forsythia was sitting and said, "If you choose to compete in the States, let me know. I could offer advice on travel and lodging."

She thanked me for the offer and said she was considering filing an application to play in the US Women's Amateur and the Women's Open. Her parents also thanked me for my interest in their daughter's career and said they thought I was an ideal partner for their daughter in Sir Harold's tournament. Choosing a partner from the British Isles could have resulted in resentment on the part of those not chosen. I appreciated their compliment and said I hoped their daughter would continue to improve and be selected for the Curtis Cup team. I told Rosie that she couldn't have a better example for a big sister than Forsythia.

Finally, I thanked Dorothy Gilroy for the hospitality shown to the players and caddies during the tournament and for the excellent dinner. There would be no Gnomewood Seven-Club Challenge without her and Sir Harold as hosts. I asked her to express my gratitude to Leffingwell, Grafton, and Soufflé.

As Dick and I were about to board the bus, Sir Harold motioned for us to step aside. He confided to us that he had purchased nearby land called Barefield Farm, a nudist colony. With that, he burst out laughing.

Dick and I looked at each other for a moment, and then Dick asked if the clientele would be the same.

"No, no," he replied. "They have moved to France, but this is strictly confidential."

Dick asked him to let us know when we could report this news. "We want a scoop."

Sir Harold waved goodbye as we boarded the bus back to the Prince Rupert.

Back at the hotel, we decided against joining some of the sportswriters in the Bear & Owl. We had notes to write up, and I would be seeing him on the morning train to London.

When the train pulled into Paddington Station, I gathered my clubs, bag, and valise and exited the train with Dick. We shook hands, and he said he hoped to see me at the Open that summer at Lytham St. Annes.

I told him I would make every effort to be there, but it depended on my editor. With that, I waved goodbye and boarded a cab to Heathrow.

I was unable to return for the Open. I had several assignments to cover baseball and the PGA tournament. However, during that time, I wondered what was going on with the development at Barefield.

CHAPTER 20

The much-anticipated letter from Sir Harold arrived during the holidays. He invited me to defend my title won last year at Gnomewood. But, if I accepted, I would be expected to play at the inauguration of Barefield, the former nudist colony that Sir Harold had acquired and turned into a nine-hole, par-3 course. Hew Fossilgrass would also be playing. He had helped design the course and selected the seed for the fairways. The other players that day would be golf writers who were less skilled than those competing in the Gnomewood Seven-Club Challenge but would like to participate in this golf outing. I accepted Sir Harold's invitation and was curious as to how challenging Barefield might be. Consequently, I wrote to Dick and asked what he knew about the new course.

Several weeks later, Dick answered my letter and wrote that he and his wife had visited Barefield. Sir Harold had shown him the progress that had been made. Greens and bunkers had been constructed, and the fairways had been seeded. The three rows of apple trees along the border by the road were left intact. In the past, the trees had guarded the sunbathers from onlookers on the road. Hew Fossilgrass would be acting as professional there. Dick concluded by saying that I would be playing with some high-handicap golfers on this inaugural round. Good luck! He added that a sign was still hanging from the clubhouse: "Bare your soul to the sun." However, the sign and the clubhouse would come down and be replaced by a new clubhouse.

When the following summer arrived, I had obtained permission to attend the Open at Muirfield. I met Dick, and we witnessed the emergence of a future star, Gary Player, from South Africa. His winning score of 284 was ten shots better than that of the defending champion, Peter Thompson. During the Open, Dick said he had visited Barefield and seen the new clubhouse. He met Leffingwell and walked several holes, observing that the greens and fairways were growing in—and the bunkers had been filled with sand. Dick seemed confident that the course would be ready to play later that summer.

After I covered three Dodgers games, the team moved to Los Angeles. I flew back to New York to spend a few days with my wife and daughter before flying to London and then on to Gnomewood-by-Sea. I met Dick at the Prince Rupert, and we caught up on our recent experiences covering sporting events. He knew I was going to play in the new Barefield tournament with some high-handicap sportswriters.

I said I could handle nine holes of wayward golf. The experience should make for amusing reading when I returned home and wrote about my Barefield adventure. Dick had spoken with Sir Harold earlier in the day, and Sir Harold had said the course was quite playable. I asked if Miss Shotwell would be playing this year, but Dick said she was playing in a lady's tournament in Croydon and planned on attending the final day of competition. There would be another lady golfer participating this year. Miss Mary O'Toole, an up-an-coming amateur, was known for having a sound game and should be a good partner.

I wanted to see Barefield, and Dick said he would call Gnomewood Links to see if Leffingwell or Grafton could drive me to view the course. Leffingwell said he would meet me outside the Prince Rupert in about fifteen minutes.

The jeep soon arrived with Leffingwell driving, and after greeting him, we drove the short distance to Barefield. The road passed the apple trees along the property and ended in the parking lot by the new clubhouse. The building was a white stucco, one-story structure with a large front porch. The starter's hut was a small wooden building by the first tee painted green. The ninth green was situated about fifty yards from the clubhouse. This distance provided a safe distance from the green so errant shots wouldn't end up on the front porch.

The course itself was relatively flat, and there were a few subtle undulations in the fairways. The rough was about two inches high and shouldn't present any great difficulty in hitting the ball. Leffingwell drove me around all nine holes, and I concluded the course was a reasonable challenge for the average golfer, but I would find out tomorrow.

As we returned to the clubhouse, Fossilgrass emerged from the doorway to welcome me. He said I would be playing tomorrow with Phloosie Archibald, and Brad Brackenfield, currently a food critic. The field would be limited to nine threesomes except one group, the Gravediggers, who wanted to play as a foursome. Fossilgrass reluctantly gave them permission to do so. Sir Harold was planning to be here tomorrow, along with the mayor and several officials from Gnomewood-by-Sea. I said I was pleased to be playing at the official opening of Barefield and looked forward to tomorrow. With that, Leffingwell and I left Barefield and returned to the Prince Rupert.

As we drove back to the hotel, I asked Leffingwell if any former members of Barefield had returned. He laughed and said, "Last month, a van showed up, and out jumped about a dozen men carrying golf clubs and asking, 'Where are the nude ladies who are supposed to caddie for us?' Fossilgrass informed them that the nudist colony had closed last year—and they were not welcome to play.

"The van driver gunned his engine and roared off, leaving an angry and confused group of men. Since Fossilgrass didn't want the men hanging around the club, he called the local sheriff and requested the men be removed as trespassers. The sheriff arrived driving a paddy wagon and shooed the former members of the nudist club into the wagon. 'Someone will pay for this,' could be heard from inside the wagon as it departed for the train station."

Leffingwell added that there had been no further episodes of former nudists returning to the club. And the golfers seeking the lady caddies were out twenty pounds in this scam. No wonder the driver of the van who dropped them off at Barefield had left so quickly.

Upon my arrival at the Prince Rupert, I went to my room and finished unpacking. I heard some voices emanating from the Bear & Owl and thought I recognized one or two. After unpacking, I ventured down to the pub and was greeted by Geoff Cloverjoy and Phil Frogwell-Potts. After handshakes, I joined them for a beer. A few minutes later, Fowler Thistletoe, Livingston Phogg-Smythe, and Bob Paltry walked in. Bob's toupee was slightly different in size and color from what he wore last year.

We finished our beer and decided it was time for dinner. We found a round table that seated six. Conversation over dinner centered on the young lady amateur invited this year, Miss Mary Catherine O'Toole. I was surprised I hadn't been informed about her by Sir Harold. Those who knew of her agreed she wasn't quite in the Forsythia Shotwell class, but she was good and nearly as long a hitter. She had a short, athletic build and a compact, powerful swing.

Thistletoe said he had covered a tournament in which Miss Shotwell and Miss O'Toole had competed—and Miss O'Toole was only a few yards shorter in driving distance. Miss Shotwell won the tournament, but it was mainly because of her putting. If Miss O'Toole had any weakness, it was in her short game and putting.

We all agreed the tournament would be more interesting with Miss O'Toole's presence. Someone asked with whom she would be paired, and they all looked at me. I replied that I had been invited to play at Barefield because I was on the winning team last year and assumed Miss Shotwell would be my partner at Gnomewood. I said I was playing at Barefield tomorrow, and I said one of my playing partners at Barefield was Brad Brackenfield.

Paltry said, "I will come over to Barefield tomorrow to watch you, and by the way, who's your caddie?"

This brought laughs from around the table. Apparently, the story had spread about naked ladies as caddies at Barefield.

The next morning at breakfast, I met the same sportswriters with whom I had dined last night. They thought I would already be at Barefield, but I said the inaugural round was not scheduled to start until eleven so golfers on the train from London would have an opportunity to warm up.

Phogg-Smythe said a bit facetiously that he wondered if a few of the writers might not know how to warm up, thinking a player simply stepped up to the first tee and fired away. I hoped this wasn't true, but I conceded to myself that he might be right. After breakfast, I enjoyed a cigarette before meeting Grafton and being driven to Barefield.

I arrived at Barefield at ten o'clock. A few golfing sportswriters had already arrived. They were a motley group. A few looked as though they had just finished typing their columns for the morning papers before arriving at Gnomewood. Their shirt collars were open, and their neckties were askew.

The bus meeting the train from London arrived and deposited a larger group. At this point, Fossilgrass emerged from the clubhouse, along with another man, and he introduced me to his new assistant, Rollo Beasley. The new assistant had worked previously at the Swales, a golf course farther down the coast. He was of a lean side with gray hair and a friendly manner. He said he had been a professional before the war and played tournament golf for a few years after the war before becoming a club professional. He looked forward to working at Barefield. He would serve as greenskeeper and give lessons to golfers new to the game.

The practice area at Barefield consisted of a chipping and putting green and a narrow strip that allowed just two players to hit to the 150-yard mark. The driving range at Gnomewood Links would be available for more advanced golfers. I noted several golfers in the practice area hitting short irons and attempting to hit the hundred-yard mark. None of them were coming close. The action on the putting green showed a few could get close to the hole. This practice would pay a greater reward than flailing away with their irons.

I recognized one golfer on the putting green. It was Phil "Phloosie" Archibald. I had met him during last year's tournament. He hung around before it started, hoping to be included in the field if someone failed to show—or if one of the writers suffered a strained back in practice and had to drop out. I walked over to meet him, and he immediately said, "Hello, champ!" We chatted briefly before the bus from the train station arrived with the rest of the field.

For the next half an hour, the golfers were sorted out as to who would be playing with whom. The list had been prepared by Sir Harold, based on their reporting ability and not on whatever golf ability they claimed. Several of the writers carried their clubs in what appeared to be shopping bags. A few had golf bags containing at least twenty clubs, and they would have to sort out which seven they would use. I decided to warm up by hitting a few wedge shots on the limited practice range.

One confused writer asked how we started the tournament, and I let Fossilgrass explain the game to him. I realized why Sir Harold had invited several extra players. He suspected there would be a few who were too bewildered and intimidated to start and finish nine holes.

I continued to watch the sportswriters warming up. A few demonstrated some ability to connect the club with the ball. I asked Beasley, the new assistant, how much time had been allotted for the nine holes.

"Not enough," he replied. Apparently, Sir Harold had suspected that, after several hours, a few players would still be trying to finish the nine holes. At that point, he or Fossilgrass would call the players in and say it was now cocktail hour.

Several sportswriters from neighboring towns asked me about Barefield and its attraction for local golfers.

I responded, "Sir Harold thought it was a good idea to construct a nine-hole par-3 course that didn't demand a great deal of skill—but still satisfied the desire to play the game. I think the course offers a good way to introduce children to golf and for women who are just taking up the game. Barefield should be open for play the day after the Gnomewood Seven-Club Tournament is finished." With that said, it was time to start.

I walked to the first tee with Fossilgrass, who was acting as starter. Phloosie Archibald and Brad Brackenfield would be playing with me and were already on the tee. Sir Harold had driven to the clubhouse on his motorcycle to greet the local reporters. I heard him say he hoped to see them playing Barefield in the future.

At eleven o'clock, I was introduced as the defending champion at Gnomewood and, along with my two partners, would be playing the initial round at Barefield. I teed up my ball and hit a 6-iron to the green. The other two hit wobbly shots just short of the green. I parred the hole, and the other two took double bogies.

Three holes at Barefield had bunkers: three, seven, and nine. On the third hole, I hit into a bunker and hit a feeble shot out, leaving a twenty-foot putt that I missed. Neither Archibald nor Brackenfield hit their tee shots far enough to reach the sand. They both bogied the hole with me. I managed three more bogies during the round, and the rest were pars. Archibald scored his only par on the fifth hole by sinking a ten-foot putt.

The ninth hole was 202 yards, and a large bunker served to catch shots that might end up in the parking lot or on the front steps of the clubhouse. I parred the hole, and the other two had double bogies. In the clubhouse, we added up our scores. I had a thirty-one, Archibald had a forty-eight, and Brackenfield had a fifty. My partners did not dwell on their bad shots, but Brackenfield realized trying to play Gnomewood Links at some future date would result in a score near one hundred— along with several lost balls.

I glanced out at the course. On the seventh hole, I saw Fossilgrass in a bunker. Another golfer was apparently giving him a lesson on playing from the sand. The player swung and lifted a cloud of sand, but I couldn't see the ball. Fossilgrass then took the club and swung, blasting the ball out near the flagstick. It was a quick lesson on bunker play.

My two partners announced their thirst, and we sat down with our beer. We were soon joined by three others who had just finished. Their scores were in the high forties, but they were enthusiastic about Barefield and hoped to play it again. I suggested we go outside to watch the golfers finish their round.

I saw Beasley walking in with two golfers, one of whom had the sack of clubs. They had apparently given up. When he saw me, he shook his head, indicating their golf was over. He escorted them into the clubhouse to temper their frustration with their favorite beverage.

Shortly, I heard a motorcycle and saw Sir Harold approaching. He waved to me as the motorcycle skidded to a stop. "All done?" he asked.

I said, "I survived and enjoyed playing Barefield, but I'm looking forward to getting back to Gnomewood."

Fossilgrass was still on the course, and Beasley said he was going to stay by the ninth hole and congratulate the golfers as they finished.

Sir Harold told me to grab my clubs and hop in the sidecar for the drive back to Gnomewood.

The trip took only a few minutes, and he dropped me in front of the Gnomewood clubhouse before he sped back to Barefield. The practice range was full of golfers preparing for tomorrow's qualifying round. I took my clubs and found a spot near the end of the range next to a young lady. I introduced myself and found I was known to her as the defending champion. She introduced herself as Mary Catherine O'Toole from Southport. She said she had been invited by Sir Harold to play in the Gnomewood Seven-Club Challenge based on her performance in the Lancashire Junior Ladies tournament at Hoylake, which she had won. Since this was a difficult course that was part of the British Open rotation, I asked what her score was.

She replied, "Eighty-one."

Dick later told me this was seven strokes better than the nearest competitor. I told her she would enjoy playing in the Gnomewood Links tournament. She told me that she hoped she could do as well as Forsythia Shotwell.

We practiced for about an hour. She was about five feet five and had a compact, quick swing. She could hammer out drives of 230–240 yards, and most were straight—with a slight draw. I thought she would be an asset to whomever she was paired with.

As she finished practice, she was met by her father, Joseph, also of a short, compact build. She introduced me to him and said he was in law enforcement in Southport. I mentioned that he would be interested in the body found during last year's tournament, but he would learn details about the investigation that followed during their stay in Gnomewood.

Miss O'Toole and her father walked back to the clubhouse, and I resumed hitting balls.

CHAPTER 21

The next morning, I awoke and saw it had been raining. I donned my rain gear in case the day would be a wet one.

At breakfast, I met several golf writers who had participated at Gnomewood last year. I sat down with Geoff Cloverjoy, Derick Marblehead, and Mel Camberwick, a previous winner of the Gnomewood 7-Club Challenge. The most frequently asked question was if I would miss Forsythia Shotwell. I replied that I had met the young lady from Southport, Miss Mary O'Toole, and was impressed at her shot-making ability.

Mel Camberwick said he had witnessed her final round at Hoylake and reaffirmed my impression of her. He added, "Her partner will have an excellent chance at winning, assuming his game holds up."

I said, "I'm sure Sir Harold will select another writer instead of me for her partner, based on his qualifying score."

After breakfast, we boarded the bus for the links. On arrival, I took my clubs from the locker room and proceeded to the practice range. Since my starting time for qualifying was ten thirty, I had plenty of time to work out a few flaws in my swing and practice putting.

Unfortunately, my practice and play didn't translate into a low-scoring round. I shot an eighty-four on a damp, wet day and was worried I wouldn't make the cut. However, I noted the scores for most of the sportswriters were in the eighties. Mel Camberwick and Derick Marblehead tied for low sportswriter at seventy-nine, but other scores were in the mid-to-high-eighties. The professionals' scores were all in the seventies, and Dr. Middlefield had a seventy-one. Miss O'Toole and two others had shot seventy-five.

At dinner, there was speculation about tomorrow's pairings. A few assumed I would have Miss O'Toole as a partner, but Dick pointed out that it was unlikely Sir Harold would pair me with an outstanding lady amateur two years in a row. Dick thought a pairing with Mel Camberwick would be hard to beat since Mel had written about her play in several tournaments. Mel was someone with whom she would feel comfortable as a partner. A few other names were mentioned, including Ian Crankshaw, but this didn't arouse much consideration.

After dinner, a few of the writers adjourned to the Bear & Owl. I decided to return to my room, and on my way, I checked the weather prediction for tomorrow. There was to be a morning squall, but it would be over by ten. This would catch the early matches, but it shouldn't affect those with later starting times. At breakfast, there was muted conversation as we were eager to catch the bus for Gnomewood Links and find out who our partners would be.

Arriving at Gnomewood, we hurried to the clubhouse to see if the pairings had been posted. Just as we arrived, Sir Harold arrived with the pairings and starting times. There were a few cheerful acknowledgments and a few groans. I noticed none of the pros were present in the clubhouse or on the range. When asked about their absence, Sir Harold said he had also posted the pairings at Foggy Shores, and the bus would be bringing the pros and caddies shortly.

Meanwhile, I saw my partner was Miss O'Toole. She had ridden to the clubhouse with Sir Harold. So much for Dick's prediction that Sir Harold wouldn't pair me with a lady golfer again. Dick was paired with Pylton Suggs, a former prizefighter from Cardiff, and Dr. Middlefield was paired with Geoff Cloverjoy.

With the arrival of the pros, there was a scramble to get clubs from the lockers and head to the practice range. Miss O'Toole said she was pleased to be paired with me, the defending champion, and I reminded her I had been paired with Miss Shotwell—and she had been the stronger member of our team. She said that I hadn't impaired Miss Shotwell's ability in any way. We decided to play the Dunlap Maxflow, the ball she was familiar with.

We were scheduled to start at ten thirty. Our opponents were Nippengay and Thinwood. After warming up, Miss O'Toole and I proceeded to the first tee, where we were joined by our opponents. Harley Bellows had a brief conversation with Miss O'Toole before announcing her name. He introduced her as a rising young talent from Southport. Miss O'Toole had the honors, took two practice swings, and belted a drive of about 230 yards down the middle. Nippengay, who had recently turned professional, followed with a drive just as long. We halved the first hole and the second. Our opponents won the par-5 third hole with a birdie; Nippengay struck a wedge that landed five feet from the flagstick, and Thinwood sank the putt. The match remained the same through the front nine. Our opponents were 1-up.

Our opponents had the honors starting on the back nine. Thinwood stood on the tenth tee, turning his head back and forth to judge the wind direction. He then teed up his ball and slammed a long drive that faded into the bunker guarding the fairway as it bent right.

I was up, and Miss O'Toole cautioned me to aim left—even if the ball landed in the lentils. This position gave a better angle to the green. I took two practice swings and stroked a drive to the left that ventured into the edge of the lentil growth. We were slightly away, and it was Miss O'Toole's shot. She found the ball, dropped it in the designated area, and smacked a 6-iron to the center of the green.

Nippengay was in the bunker, and after several practice swings, he blasted out to about forty yards short of the green. This left Thinwood with a difficult pitch shot. He changed clubs several times, debating whether to use a wedge or short iron and play a low, running shot to the green. He finally decided on a wedge, and then he stroked a shot that landed about halfway to the green. His partner then lofted a wedge to the green about ten feet from the flag. It was their fourth shot. I now had a birdie putt of about twelve feet that broke an inch outside the hole. We lined it up, and I rolled a good putt that just missed on the low side. Our short par putt was conceded, and the match was now even.

The eleventh hole was 212 yards, with lettuce on the right and two bunkers guarding the left side of the green. Miss O'Toole used a 3-iron that landed just short of the green. Nippengay also hit a 3-iron, but his shot landed on the left edge of the green and rolled into a bunker.

Approaching the hole, we determined I was away. Using my putter from off the green, I stroked a putt about five feet short of the cup. As Thinwood entered the bunker to play his shot, I wondered if he was a bit unsettled by his stubbed wedge shot on the previous hole. I could hear Nippengay giving him advice about blasting out of the bunker. After several practice swings, he exploded out over the flagstick, landing on the far edge of the green. Their next shot was a twenty-footer for par that Nippengay ran by the cup several feet.

Miss O'Toole was now away, and after determining the line, she stroked in the five-footer for par, putting us 1-up.

The twelfth hole was halved, and it was on to thirteen, a short par-3, with a deep bunker behind the green. I reminded Miss O'Toole that the breeze was behind us, and the main danger on this hole was having the ball end up in the back bunker.

She acknowledged my warning and selected an 8-iron. Her tee shot landed just short of the green.

Nippengay then hit a short iron that landed on the back of the green but held, leaving Thinwood with a difficult downhill putt of about ten feet.

I was away and decided to chip the ball. I used an 8-iron and left the ball about four feet below the cup.

Thinwood lined up his downhill putt and ran it by about eight feet. Nippengay missed his putt for a bogie.

Miss O'Toole then sank the four-footer for par and a win. We were now 2-up.

The fourteenth hole was halved with bogies. Thinwood and I drove into the mustard. Our partners shots from the drop area were at least one hundred yards short of the green, and Thinwood and I hit poor approach shots that missed the green. Neither side could save par.

The fifteenth hole was a 185-yard par-3. The green is guarded by pot bunkers on the right and left and a large bunker behind the green. Miss O'Toole's tee shot landed in the right bunker, and Nippengay's tee shot landed in the left bunker.

I was away and blasted out a shot that barely cleared the lip of the bunker, leaving about a fifteen-foot putt.

Thinwood blasted out a shot that landed about twenty-five feet from the flagstick.

Nippengay was first to putt. He stroked a putt that stopped about a foot from the cup.

Miss O'Toole had a par-saving putt to win the hole. We both thought it broke about an inch to the right. She lined it up, took two practice strokes, and sank it. We won the hole and were dormie. At that point, I didn't think there was anything wrong with her putting.

Sixteen was a 400-yard par-4, playing downwind. Miss O'Toole and I realized the real danger was the gaping bunker behind the green. I decided to hit a drive aimed right. If it faded, it would land in the peas. Using a 5-wood, I lofted a drive that the wind carried some 220 yards.

Thinwood used his driver and hit a slice that traveled beyond the pea patch into relatively deep rough.

Next to hit was Miss O'Toole. She struck a 6-iron that carried to the base of the green.

Nippengay found his partner's drive in the rough and had to play a wedge shot back to the fairway. Thinwood then faced a short iron shot to the green. He lofted a shot that carried to the back of the green. Nippengay was faced with a downhill putt of some twenty feet. His putt rolled some ten feet beyond the hole. Thinwood was away, and he stroked a putt that came up two feet short. With that, he picked up their ball and conceded the hole, realizing even if we took three putts and halved the hole with a bogie, we would win three and two. Handshakes followed, and our opponents admitted they weren't up to our level of play.

Miss O'Toole's father rushed up to congratulate us. He had been following our match from a distance and said he sometimes made his daughter nervous if she recognized him in the gallery. He added, "She has gained more experience playing in tournaments, and this is no longer a problem."

We walked to the clubhouse, and Mr. O'Toole ordered a ginger ale for Mary. Several players were relaxing after their matches. Dr. Middlefield was on his second gin and tonic as he recounted his match—with Cloverjoy as his partner—against Dedmon and Bumly.

Before the match, Bumly told Cloverjoy and me about his new book on escaping from sand by chipping or putting. He said he intended to use these two methods against us in our match. Twice during the match, he attempted to demonstrate his prowess by using an 8-iron to chip from the bunker guarding the green on the eighth hole. Two strokes later, his partner, Dedmon, walked off the green, conceding the hole. Then on twelve, he attempted to putt from the bunker guarding the green on the right. He did escape on the second stroke, but the hole was already lost to par. He and Dedmon lost six and five. I looked around the room to see if Bumly or Dedmon was present, they weren't.

I couldn't help but ask the doctor if he was still using the pep pills I had observed him taking last year. He said he had stopped, but there were times when he felt he could have used them. He mentioned reports of an addicting quality to their use, and he believed his putting was better when he didn't use them. He jokingly added that his wife periodically searched his pockets, looking for Dexedrine.

Cliff Halestork was on the putting green, and I asked him about his match with the two Scotsmen since they would be our opponents tomorrow.

He replied, "They can out drive you—so don't be intimidated."

I replied, "Apparently, you haven't watched Miss O'Toole on the practice range. I think she can match Feathershanks in distance or nearly so, and I'll keep up with Crankshaw." I admitted to myself that maybe I was boasting a bit, but I didn't think lack of distance would decide our match.

Halestork wished us good luck before returning to his putting.

CHAPTER 22

I caught the bus back to the Prince Rupert, glanced in the Bear & Owl, and saw a few players enjoying beer or whiskey. The room was accumulating smoke, and I decided to head for my room for a shower and change of clothes.

Later, at dinner, I heard the usual complaints about the green speed, the rough in the drop zones, and the unpredictable breeze.

Dick joined us after working on his driving. Miss O'Toole had also been practicing. Several pros offered to match their drives with her—using their 3-woods—but she outdrove them using her driver. When the pros switched to their drivers, they managed to outdrive her—but only by ten or fifteen yards. Byf Barleycroft was the longest, followed by Nippengay and Suggs, and they were all quite complimentary in their appraisal of her driving ability.

I went to bed that night confident of our ability to compete tomorrow.

At breakfast, I shared a table with Dick and Ian Crankshaw. Although Crankshaw would be my opponent that morning, our discussion was amicable. He hoped I could attend the Great Northern Masters during one of my trips to Scotland. "Even though the courses—Nairn and Royal Dornoch—are at a northern latitude, the fairways are lush, and all you need to be comfortable is a good Scottish wool sweater."

I replied, "I hope to have my wife and daughter accompany me on one of my assignments and see Scotland and its beautiful links courses."

As we left for the bus, Dick told Ian that he hoped his partner, Feathershanks, had not had any fortification with his breakfast. Ian laughed and glanced in the Bear & Owl. The bus was waiting, and he resisted having a distilled product from Scotland.

I arrived at the clubhouse, changed to my golf shoes, grabbed my clubs, and walked to the practice range. At the far end, I saw Miss O'Toole and her father. Mary was wearing a bright green sweater and dark gray skirt.

Mr. O'Toole greeted me with a firm handshake.

Mary said, "Watch this," and she hammed a drive beyond the 250-yard marker.

I told her that she looked like she was ready to take on the Scotsmen.

I took several balls from a pile and started to practice wedge and 8-iron shots.

Within a few minutes, I heard Feathershanks's voice. He and Crankshaw were setting up practice beside us. I sensed some gamesmanship with their move. Feathershanks proceeded to hit his wedge, but Crankshaw wanted to continue our conversation at breakfast about Scottish courses farther down the northeast coast: Panmure, Montrose, and Carnoustie.

I said I had covered the Open at Carnoustie, won by Ben Hogan, and hoped to play it someday. With that said, I turned and resumed hitting balls.

Several minutes later, Feathershanks paused his practice and walked over to where he could observe Miss O'Toole practicing. "That's a strong grip you're using, young lady."

Mr. O'Toole immediately stepped between Mary and Feathershanks and said, "The grip's done her fine—no need to change!"

Feathershanks muttered something to Mr. O'Toole before turning to where he and Crankshaw were practicing.

Miss O'Toole and I finished warming up and walked over to the putting green. On the way to the putting green, I paused briefly to say hello to Dr. Middlefield—he was practicing with his partner, Cloverjoy—and then wished Dick good luck. He said he and Pylton Suggs would need it since they were facing Peebles and Camberwick in their match.

We were able to practice putting before the Scotsmen joined us on the green. Crankshaw appeared to be missing putts on the right, and I felt reassured that Miss O'Toole and I would be competitive—at least on the greens.

Harley Bellows arrived on the first tee and walked over to meet Miss O'Toole. They chatted for a few minutes before he walked back to the tee. It was nearly time to start, and I mentioned to Mary that we should move up to the first tee. We were joined by the two Scotsmen.

A small gallery had assembled to witness the start of the day's play, and Mary had the honors.

Bellows announced, "Teeing off is Miss Mary O'Toole, recent winner of the Lancashire Ladies Junior Match-Play tournament. Her partner was on last year's winning team, Mr. John Nelson."

Applause and a few cheers greeted us, and Mary waved to the small crowd and then teed up the ball. She proceeded to slam a drive of about 240 yards down the left-center of the fairway.

Feathershanks then stepped to the tee. He and his partner both wore dark gray plus fours with argyle stockings and light blue sweaters. Feathershanks then blasted a drive of some 260 yards into the artichokes along the right side of the fairway.

Approaching Miss O'Toole's drive, I elected to hit a 6-iron. After two practice strokes, I smacked a shot to the base of the green.

Crankshaw found his partner's drive in the artichokes and took a drop in the drop area. He played a midiron that missed the green on the left. Feathershanks next played a chip shot to about two feet from the pin.

Miss O'Toole then rolled a putt of about twenty feet to about a foot from the pin. Both remaining putts were conceded.

The second and third holes were halved with par. The par-3 fourth hole was halved with bogies, after Crankshaw and I drove into bunkers. Our partners hit explosion shots that left us with five- and six-foot putts that we both missed. The fifth hole was halved with par, and it was on to the sixth hole. I knew from last year that it was best to drive away from the danger of the elephant grass on the left and aim toward the carrots on the right. My drive traveled some 230 yards to the edge of the carrots. Crankshaw hit his drive into the carrots, requiring his partner to drop beside the green-and-white stake.

Miss O'Toole was away, and she lofted a midiron that drifted into one of the pot bunkers right of the green. Feathershanks was next to play, and he hit a midiron to the center of the green.

I had a decent lie in the bunker, but I needed to explode out to clear the top of the bunker and then hope the ball would stop near the flagstick. Unfortunately, my first attempt failed to clear the edge—and the ball rolled back into the bunker.

Miss O'Toole had to play our third shot. She blasted out to about ten feet from the flag.

Crankshaw was now up, and he rolled a putt to about four feet from the cup.

I had to make the ten-footer to salvage bogie. I missed the putt, and Feathershanks paused to see if we would concede their four-foot par putt.

Mary and I both shook our heads no—even though our opponents were almost certain to win the hole.

Feathershanks stepped up and sank the four-foot putt. As he walked off the green, he said, "A Scotsman doesn't miss those four-footers."

Our opponents were now 1-up.

The seventh and eighth holes were halved, and we now faced the par-5 ninth hole. Feathershanks's driving ability came forth, and he blasted a tee shot of close to 280 yards.

Miss O'Toole followed with a drive of close to 240 yards that hooked into the left rough.

I had a reasonable lie and used my 5-wood to hit a shot of about 210 yards into the eggplant on the right, which left us a good sixty yards from the green.

Crankshaw was now up, and he stroked a 3-wood some 220 yards down the fairway.

Miss O'Toole had to play a shot from the drop zone, using an 8-iron, and her shot landed on the green and rolled off to the left.

Feathershanks was next to hit, and he stroked a wedge to about five feet from the flag.

I was away and faced with a wedge shot from rough that was several inches high. After several practice strokes, I punched a shot that barely landed on the green and rolled about twenty feet from the flag.

Miss O'Toole was away, and her putt just missed to the right.

Our opponents now had two putts to win the hole. Crankshaw rolled a good putt a few inches short, and we conceded their remaining putt. We were now 2-down.

At the refreshment card between the ninth green and tenth tee, our opponents seemed quite confident in victory. Crankshaw and Feathershanks selected bottles of soda water to which Feathershanks added the contents from a flask to each bottle.

Miss O'Toole and I had apple cider and a cookie. I got a whiff of the contents from the flask and asked what the brand was.

"Wild Deer," Feathershanks replied. "Seven years old." He didn't offer me any, and I wouldn't have accepted his offer.

After about ten minutes, we resumed play. I was wondering when the effects of our opponents' premature celebration would take effect. We didn't have long to wait. On the eleventh hole, a 212-yard par-3, Feathershanks hit a sharp hook that almost landed on the tenth tee. Miss O'Toole hit a 3-iron to the base of the green. Crankshaw responded to his partner's hook by smacking a wedge short of the green into a bunker. From there, Feathershanks hit a weak explosion shot that barely reached the green. Our opponents were still away. Crankshaw stroked a putt that traveled about six feet beyond the cup.

I was next to play, and I stroked a putt to about two feet from the hole. Feathershanks looked at our putt and then conceded the hole. We were now 1-down.

The twelfth hole was halved with par. Feathershanks managed to sink a fifteen-foot putt for par. We won the short par-3 thirteenth hole when Feathershanks hit his tee shot into the deep bunker behind the hole.

Crankshaw attempted to explode the ball out, but he failed. The ball advanced to the side of the bunker. Feathershanks blasted the ball out, but it clipped the lip of the bunker and landed on the edge of the green. They were still away.

Miss O'Toole's tee shot landed about ten feet from the pin, and Crankshaw was now hitting their fourth shot, a twenty-foot downhill putt. He stroked a putt that ran about ten feet by the cup. It was decided we were away. I stroked a putt that rolled over the right lip and stopped a few inches above the cup. Our opponents conceded this par putt, and the match was now even.

The fourteenth hole was a 517-yard par-5 alight dogleg left, with a growth of mustard paralleling the fairway on the right.

Miss O'Toole cautioned me to try to stay left and avoid the mustard because, if I hit into the mustard, the grass by the drop zone was at least three inches high. I felt confident I could hit a draw, and I did. The ball landed about 230 yards down the fairway.

Crankshaw was next to play. He hammered a drive of some 250 yards that sliced into the mustard. A five-minute search failed to reveal the ball, and rather than search more and damage the mustard, our opponents used the local rule of dropping the ball in the drop area.

Feathershanks played a 3-wood out of the grass, but the ball only traveled about 180 yards down the fairway.

Miss O'Toole then slammed a 3-wood about 220 yards, leaving me with a wedge to the green.

Next to hit was Crankshaw. He struck a short-iron that just missed the green on the right. I judged my wedge shot would be affected by the breeze off the coast, and I played a shot to the left of the flag that landed about six feet from the flag.

Feathershanks was away, and after getting down on his hands and knees to evaluate his putt, he struck the putt about three feet beyond the hole.

Miss O'Toole had a six-foot birdie putt that she calmly rolled in for a win. We were now 1-up.

On the fifteenth hole, a par-3, our opponents each took a swig from Feathershanks's flask.

Crankshaw winked at me and said, "We needed some refreshment."

Miss O'Toole was on the tee. She smacked a midiron that landed just short of the green.

Feathershanks then blasted a 6-iron into a pot bunker guarding the green on the left.

I thought, *Crankshaw hasn't had much success from bunkers, and this upcoming shot from a bunker probably won't help their team. I wonder if Mary is playing short to save me from having to play a difficult shot from the sand.*

As it turned out, we parred the hole—and our opponents took three putts from where Crankshaw's poor bunker shot landed. We were now 2-up.

The sixteenth hole was a 400-yard par-4 playing downwind. A potato patch guarded the green on the right, and there was a large, deep bunker behind the green. I wanted to aim down the middle, but my tee shot landed just off the fairway on the right, short of the potatoes.

Crankshaw hit one of his better drives, landing down the middle.

Miss O'Toole followed with a 6-iron to the green.

Feathershanks hit the green with their second shot, leaving ten-to-twelve-foot birdie putts for Crankshaw and myself. I was slightly away. Miss O'Toole and I lined up my putt; it broke slightly to the right. I stroked the putt on exactly the line we had decided on for a birdie.

Crankshaw and Feathershanks surveyed their putt from all angles before Crankshaw took his stance. He stroked a good putt, but I could see it would break below the hole, which it did. We won the hole and the match. We shook hands with our opponents, and then I tipped my cap to the applauding gallery. Mary's father rushed up to hug her—as did several others who had traveled from Southport to watch her play.

We walked back to the clubhouse. I was too tired to walk back to the holes we had just finished to see how Dick and his partner stood in their match against Harry Vardon Taylor and Derick Marblehead.

Mary and her father had a ginger ale before selecting a ham and cheese sandwich. They then settled on a couch facing the links. I took a sausage sandwich and a beer and then walked out on the veranda to wait for the incoming players. I saw Dick and his partner, Suggs, walking in. They must have finished on fifteen or sixteen. Behind them were Taylor and Marblehead. Marblehead's slumped shoulders told me they had probably been defeated.

Upon reaching the clubhouse, Dick spotted me and said, "We won, but we were lucky. Taylor outdrove us by twenty yards, but he couldn't putt through an open barn door. Marblehead couldn't sink every four-, five-, and six-foot putt he was left with. Our opponents would go one up and then lose a hole. On the back nine, they lost three straight holes before finally parring thirteen for a half; they lost two more, and we won."

Suggs paused as they had walked in and found out from a spectator that the doctor and Cloverjoy were leading in their match. He joined Dick in the clubhouse and said their opponent tomorrow would probably be the doctor and Whiffy. Upon hearing this, I realized Cloverjoy's nickname had stuck.

Dick and I took a beer and moved to the veranda to watch the incoming players. The yellow outfit of Paltry and the red slacks of Barleycroft appeared, and judging from their jaunty walk, I guessed they had won. Trudging behind them were Frogwell-Potts and Andy Quickfoot.

Paltry left Barleycroft and entered the clubhouse. He saw Dick and me on the veranda and said, "Barleycroft and I will see you and the young lady tomorrow." With that, he walked back into the clubhouse for some refreshment.

When the doctor and Cloverjoy appeared, they were engaged in an animated conversation. The smiles on their faces made me assume they had been victorious. Thus, the semifinal matches for tomorrow would be Miss O'Toole and me against Paltry and Barleycroft; the other was Dick and Pylton Suggs facing the doctor and Cloverjoy. I thought the teams would be evenly matched and provide the gallery with an entertaining golfing event.

At dinner, I shared a table with Paltry, Cloverjoy, Phogg-Smythe, Camberwick, Frogwell-Potts, and Dick. I said, "We are dining with some of our competition, which is something unique in the sporting world. Most athletic teams stay in separate hotels or in different wings of a motel. In the early days of our PGA Tour, some players shared a car and even a hotel room to save money. They frequently dined together and enjoyed entertainment provided by the host city—or even by the pros themselves. To me, the outstanding example of this was the tournament sponsored by Bing Crosby. After dinner, a successful pro, Jimmy Demerit, would sing a solo or duet with Bing. Crosby would then say, 'If I had your golf game, I would give up singing.' Demerit would counter by saying, 'If I had your voice, I would give up chasing the little white ball.'"

Talk then turned to match play and how some golfers seemed to rise to the competition, while playing at a mundane level in a medal play tournament. I mentioned how the American professional, Walter Hagen, dominated match play in our PGA tournament over several years. Hagen was something of a showman and enjoyed the nightlife, although this was often exaggerated. One reporter followed Hagen during a tournament and observed, at a cocktail party, how Hagen would appear to be enjoying several highballs, but he would cleverly dump half the drink in a nearby plant when he didn't think anyone was watching. As the party broke up, fellow pros and host club members would marvel at Hagen's capacity for liquor. His opponent would assume Walter would be hungover the next day and not play his best. Hagen would be at the top of his game on these occasions and catch his opponent by surprise. During another tournament, Hagen arrived in a rented limousine, wearing formal dress, accompanied by two young actresses, leaving the impression he had experienced a night on the town and was in no condition to play championship golf. Again, this ploy was intended to weaken the competitiveness of the opposition.

The name of Walter Hagen prompted Bob Paltry to recall Henry Cotton, a British golf professional. Cotton was an admirer of Hagen, and as a successful tournament professional, he was known to wear tailored clothing and, later in life, drive a Rolls-Royce. He married the daughter of a wealthy businessman in Buenos Aires, and she acquired the nickname of "Toots." Together, they shared a standard of living well above that of the average golf professional.

As the party broke up, Frogwell-Potts motioned me over to a corner of the dining room. He asked if I would be willing to go along with a stunt he had conceived while hearing about Walter Hagen. Would I be willing to arrive at the clubhouse in the jeep, driven by Grafton, in which there would be two young actresses who had arrived by train from London that morning before the tournament started. I would have an open bottle of champagne and give the impression I had been partying all night.

I said the idea was interesting, but I was not Walter Hagen and needed time in the morning to warm up. Plus, I owed it to Miss O'Toole to be ready to play my best.

Frogwell said he understood and that he might stage such an arrival himself next year.

CHAPTER 23

The next morning was cloudy and blustery, and I decided to wear a sweater and a windbreaker.

At the breakfast table, conversation centered around how Miss O'Toole would fare against stiffer competition than what she had faced in the past.

Bob Paltry, wearing his bumblebee outfit, said he and Barleycroft would give us a good match and that Miss O'Toole and I should expect to follow them, as spectators, in the final match.

I replied, "The young lady is already tournament tested—maybe not to the extent of my partner last year, Miss Shotwell—but I think we can hold our own today."

Joining us at the table were Dick, Geoff Cloverjoy, Frogwell-Potts, and Fowler Thistletoe. Frogwell-Potts again brought up his idea of having me arrive in the jeep accompanied by two young actresses—with an open bottle of champagne—leaving the impression I had been partying that night.

Paltry immediately said, "If that were to happen, Barleycroft and I will be 1-up before the tournament starts."

We all agreed Frogwell-Potts should be the one to stage his arrival. Cloverjoy said his partner, Dr. Middlefield, could come close to staging such an act. He would mention it to him.

We finished breakfast, caught the bus, and arrived at the clubhouse. Miss O'Toole and her father were already on the practice range. I quickly changed to my golf shoes and headed for the range to join her. Her father eyed me and asked if I had behaved myself last night. I said I had experienced a dull evening in the company of my fellow golfers. He replied that he just wanted to know.

Arriving on the practice range were Dick, his partner, Pylton Suggs, and Cloverjoy. A few minutes later, Paltry and Barleycroft showed up. They made a colorful pair with Barleycroft's red slacks and Paltry's black-and-yellow outfit. We all began practicing in earnest. Miss O'Toole had already progressed from short irons to her 6-iron.

As starting time approached, we moved to the practice putting green. After hitting a few putts, I judged the speed on the green was about the same as yesterday and should be about the same on the links. Members of the other semifinal match, Whistle and Suggs against Cloverjoy and Dr. Middlefield, were still on the range.

A gallery of perhaps seventy-five to one hundred, plus a few stray dogs, had gathered by the first tee. I heard the jeep pull up by the first tee and sensed Sir Harold was arriving.

A few minutes later, a horn blew, indicating starting time was near and the players in the first match should move to the teeing area.

Sir Harold and Harley Bellows were standing by the first tee, and they greeted our group as we arrived.

Miss O'Toole would have the honors. Her father stood alongside her with the golf bag and pulled out her driver. Brief applause and a few cheers accompanied her as she teed up her ball, took several practice swings, and then smacked a drive of some 230 yards down the middle.

Barleycroft strode to the tee and said, "Her drive was acceptable—but watch this!" He teed up his ball, and after two wicked practice swings, he slammed a wild hook that barely stayed in bounds. I had seen his hook before, but this tee shot stayed in bounds.

We walked to our partners' tee shots.

Miss O'Toole turned to Barleycroft and said, "I think you are away, but we'll wait until you find your ball."

After several minutes, the ball was found.

I signaled that I was going to hit, and then I struck a 6-iron to the right side of the green, maybe twelve feet from the flag.

Paltry was now ready to hit. He flailed at the tall grass, and the ball landed in the rough.

Barleycroft now had to play from the rough. Although the grass near the fairway was two to three inches in length, he used what appeared to be a short iron and blasted a shot that landed on the green and bounced into a bunker to the right of the green.

Paltry, in the bunker, was now hitting four. He exploded out to about fifteen feet from the flagstick.

Miss O'Toole approached the balls on the green and promptly said, "I think you are away."

Barleycroft turned his back to the flagstick for a few seconds, turned and addressed his putt, and then ran it by at least four feet. He then smacked his ball off the green toward the second tee.

Mr. O'Toole laughed and said, "He played out of turn—you and John win." He gave Mary a hug before we joined our opponents on the second tee.

The second hole was halved, and it was on to the 505-yard third hole. Miss O'Toole was on the tee, and she hammered a drive close to 240 yards that landed at the edge of the beets, on the right.

Barleycroft was less boastful as he stood on the tee, but he turned to his partner and said, "How about 250 yards down the middle?" With that, he blasted a drive that landed in the second bunker guarding the left side of the fairway, at about 250 yards.

As we approached our drives, I could see I had a good lie and could use my 5-wood for my next shot. I was clearly away and took a smooth swing that produced a shot that landed about thirty yards from the green.

Paltry was in the bunker and was using a long iron to escape. After several practice swings, he smacked a shot that just cleared the lip of the bunker and faded into one of the pot bunkers, just short of the green.

Miss O'Toole was next to play and used her wedge to strike a shot that landed in the middle of the green.

Meanwhile, Barleycroft had climbed into the relatively deep pot bunker and managed to blast out well beyond the flag.

On the green, Paltry was away, about twenty-five feet from the hole, and he stroked a putt that came up about four feet short.

I had a fifteen-foot putt that broke left to right about two inches outside the hole. I lined it up and rolled a good putt that ended up about a foot and a half below the hole. Our opponents circled their putt several times, waiting to see if we would concede, but I told them to putt it. Barleycroft missed the par putt, and then they indicated that we should putt.

Miss O'Toole calmly stroked in our short par putt. We were now 2-up.

We halved the short par-3 fourth hole and par-4 fifth hole. The sixth hole had been a troublesome hole for golfers during the Gnomewood tournament, and today was no exception. I was on the tee and hit into the carrots, but this gave Mary a decent shot from the drop area.

Paltry's tee shot sliced beyond the growth of carrots and into deep rough. From the rough, Barleycroft managed to blast out to the fairway, leaving Paltry one hundred yards from the green.

Miss O'Toole was next to play, and she smacked a midiron to about twelve feet from the flagstick.

Paltry then played a midiron to about fifteen feet from the flag.

On the green, Barleycroft had to sink the fifteen-footer to save par. He struck a putt that just missed on the left.

We had two putts to win the hole. I putted about a foot from the cup, and after Barleycroft surveyed the one-footer, he conceded the putt. We were now 3-up, and we remained 3-up through the front nine.

The tenth hole was a par-4 dogleg right, and Miss O'Toole reminded me the hole was playing downwind—and my 5-wood would leave her with a midiron to the green. "Avoid the bunker where the fairway bends right."

I easily struck my 5-wood to about 220 yards down the fairway.

Paltry then smacked a drive that faded into the bunker—just what he didn't want to do. I could hear Barleycroft scolding Paltry as we walked down the fairway.

Miss O'Toole was away, and she stroked a 6-iron to the base of the green.

Barleycroft now had a difficult shot from the bunker; the ball had rolled near the edge, making a midiron shot nearly impossible. He gambled, using a 6-iron that clipped the lip of the bunker, and the ball traveled about fifty yards down the fairway. Paltry then hit a midiron to the right edge of the green, leaving a putt of some forty feet.

I had about a twenty-foot putt to the flag that I rolled to about a foot beyond the hole.

Barleycroft then had the forty-footer for par. The putt raced by the cup some three feet, and our opponents conceded our short putt. We were now 4-up.

The eleventh hole was a 212-yard par-3 playing into the wind. Miss O'Toole used a 3-iron that hooked into the bunker guarding the left side of the green. Barleycroft then struck a beautiful 3-iron that landed in the center of the green. I played a poor explosion shot from the bunker that barely reached the putting surface. Paltry then putted to about a foot from the hole. Miss O'Toole had a thirty-footer that she stroked to about a foot from the hole. We then conceded our opponents' short putt, and we were now 3-up.

We halved the par-4 twelfth hole and moved on to thirteen, a short par-3 with a deep bunker behind the green.

On the tee, Miss O'Toole said, "Watch Barleycroft hit his tee shot. It will ride the wind and land in the bunker." That's exactly what happened. His tee shot landed on the back edge of the green and disappeared into the bunker. Miss O'Toole then teed up her ball and hit a soft 8-iron to the base of the green. She and I walked to the side of the green to watch Paltry try to blast out. The ball was sitting up, and I thought he had a good chance of escaping. Under Barleycroft's coaching, he took several practice swings before swinging mightily and exploded the ball out to where our ball was at the base of the green.

There was a brief discussion about who was away, but it was determined that I should putt first. I noticed Barleycroft standing behind me to see what line my putt would take. I gave the putt a firm stroke and ran the putt by about a foot and a half.

Barleycroft took his stance and hit his par putt two feet beyond the hole. They asked if we would concede their bogie putt, and we did—but they refused to concede Miss O'Toole's short par putt. She calmly sank it, and we were 4-up again.

The 517-yard fourteenth played into the wind. Both Paltry and I hit weak tee shots. Our partners then used their 3-wood to advance their balls down the fairway. Miss O'Toole's shot landed in the mustard, and Barleycroft's landed in a fairway bunker. This left Paltry and me with midirons to the green, and we both missed the green. Ultimately, the hole was halved with bogies. The match was now dormie. As I walked to the fifteenth tee, I again noted the plaque commemorating Sir Harold's capture of the German submarine.

The 185-yard fifteenth hole was playing downwind, and Miss O'Toole used a 3-iron to hit a shot that the wind carried to the center of the green.

Barleycroft saw what club Miss O'Toole had used and decided he would use a midiron—a five or six—for his tee shot. He took a vigorous swing and hit a shot that landed just short of the green.

Walking to the green, I could see I would have about a twenty-five-foot putt.

Paltry would have a chip shot of maybe fifty feet. Paltry surveyed his shot and selected his wedge to loft the ball to the hole. After several practice swings, he addressed the ball, swung, and hit the turf several inches behind the ball. The shot came up short of the green, and the gallery groaned.

Barleycroft then lined up his shot and, using a short-iron, played a chip shot that landed by the flagstick and rolled some six feet beyond the hole. They marked their ball and removed the flag.

I lined up my twenty-footer and nearly sank it, leaving a tap-in and a win five and three. Our opponents congratulated us, saying we played well but were lucky today.

There was appreciative applause from the gallery, and they quickly walked back to the fourteenth green to watch the match with Dick and Suggs against Dr. Middlefield and Cloverjoy.

Miss O'Toole, her father, and I walked back to the clubhouse, and I felt a sense of relief and fatigue. We sat down at a table and waited for someone to bring us the fish chowder, crackers, and a beverage. Miss O'Toole and I had ginger ale, and Mr. O'Toole ordered a beer.

I noticed a crowd gathering outside the clubhouse. Leffingwell stood guard at the door to allow only the participants and their families inside. Mary saw two of her friends from Southport outside and asked Leffingwell if they could come inside. He opened the door, and there was a rush inside of about a dozen friends of the O'Tooles'. I got up from the table and took my soup to a corner to get some rest. Miss O'Toole and her father were now engulfed with friends and fans from her hometown.

I finished my soup and hoped to take a short nap, but suddenly there was double the noise around the clubhouse as the other match had completed. I thought I should have followed Dick in his match or waited by the fifteenth tee to catch up on how he and Suggs stood, but I was too tired, and knowing we had another match to play today, I wanted to rest in the clubhouse.

The doctor and Cloverjoy barged inside, and the doctor headed for the bar and ordered two whiskey and sodas. He took one for himself and handed the other to his caddie, Bobby Clambourne. Cloverjoy saw me resting in the corner and asked if he could join me.

I said, "Of course. Grab a bowl of chowder and whatever beverage you wish."

He returned, juggling the chowder and beer, and sat down across from me.

I asked how their match had gone and he told me that he and the doctor had won on seventeen when Suggs snap-hooked into the spinach and Mr. Whistle's 3-wood landed in the bunker guarding the green on the right. The doctor's drive penetrated the breeze and landed about 260 yards down the fairway. He hit his best 3-iron of the match to the base of the green, and two putts later, they won the match 2-up.

I said, "Miss O'Toole and I were fortunate to have a four-shot cushion going into fifteen. We won that hole and the match."

Sir Harold pulled up outside the clubhouse and announced that two food carts would be arriving shortly. He went inside and shooed the visitors from the clubhouse. The noise in the clubhouse abated somewhat as they left.

Cloverjoy was looking out at the practice range since the doctor had left shortly after downing his whiskey and soda.

I reminded him that the doctor usually showed up shortly before a match was to begin.

Cloverjoy said he knew this, but he would feel more confident about the match with the doctor present to offer advice during practice.

Dick walked over to where we were sitting and wished us luck and to play well. He added that he would probably join our group on the back nine; he was tired from his morning match against Cloverjoy and the doctor.

I saw Miss O'Toole and her father as the well-wishers left, and I told Cloverjoy I would see him on the first tee.

Mary and her father appeared invigorated by their friends and relatives from home. I glanced at my watch and saw it was one thirty, and I suggested we head for the practice range. Her father agreed and went to pick up her clubs from the locker area.

As we left the clubhouse, we were surrounded by a gallery of at least a hundred people. They followed us to the practice range, and we began to warm up.

Cloverjoy joined us and walked to the opposite end of the range. The roar from the Dr.'s Jaguar indicated his arrival. The four of us practiced for about fifteen minutes and spent the last few minutes with our drivers.

Miss O'Toole was hitting the ball solidly, but I could not hit the ball much beyond 220 yards. I felt a slight panic, but there wasn't much I could do. I didn't want to ask Mary's advice and interrupt her practice.

We walked over to the putting green and saw the doctor and Clambourne practicing. Clambourne was holding the putter blade back as the doctor hesitated to release it. I had read that this practice was designed to cure the yips. I didn't know if this would be a problem for the doctor during our match, but I thought we shouldn't concede any putt of the doctor's longer than two feet. On our way to the first tee, I mentioned this observation to Miss O'Toole and her father, and they agreed with me.

At two o'clock, Sir Harold blew a horn to indicate the final match was about to begin.

Harley Bellows, resplendent in red blazer and blue-and-white checkered slacks, was waiting on the first tee. He introduced Miss O'Toole as "a promising young amateur who was earning a reputation as a tough competitor." Generous applause greeted her as a few more fans from her hometown joined the gallery.

Miss O'Toole took several practice swings before teeing up her ball, and then she smacked a drive of some 230 yards that hooked into the left rough. I thought, *I can escape from there—no harm done.*

The doctor was introduced to generous applause—his fans who followed his play in professional tournaments were present to support him—and tipped his visor to the gallery, teed up his ball, and blasted a drive of some 280 yards down the middle. And off we went.

I found our ball in the rough. It was partially buried in grass, but I thought I could get the clubface on it and strike it on or near the green. Using my 6-iron, I punched the ball out of the rough down the fairway to the left of the green.

Cloverjoy was next to hit. He used a short-iron and hit a shot that landed at the base of the green, leaving a putt of about twenty feet.

Miss O'Toole had a chip shot from the left rough of about thirty feet from the flagstick. She used a wedge and hit a good shot, but the grass took some of the backspin off the ball—and it rolled about twelve feet beyond the hole.

The doctor was away, and he stroked a putt that rolled over the right lip of the cup and stopped a few inches beyond. We conceded this short putt.

I had a twelve-footer that was straight to the hole, but I pulled it slightly and missed to the left. We were now 1-down.

We halved the second hole and moved on to the 503-yard third. Dr. Middlefield had the honors, and he powered a drive of close to 280 yards down the middle.

Miss O'Toole followed with a drive of 235 yards down the fairway on the left, and I struck a 5-wood a little over two hundred yards.

Cloverjoy hammered a 3-wood about 220 yards that landed just short of the green.

For our next shot, Miss O'Toole struck an 8-iron that landed about eight feet from the flag.

The doctor was next up, and he chipped the ball to about five feet from the flag.

My birdie putt rimmed the cup and ran by about a foot.

Cloverjoy now had a birdie putt to win the hole. His putt was online, but it stopped several inches short. We conceded this. He and the doctor looked at our one-footer for several seconds before conceding it.

The par-3 fourth hole was halved with par despite Cloverjoy and me hitting into the cabbage, leaving our partners with difficult pitch shots from the drop area. Their pitch shots landed within two feet from the cup, and the resulting putts were conceded. The gallery applauded the par-saving shots from the cabbage drop zone.

The fifth hole was halved with par.

Both teams knew the danger on the sixth hole, and Cloverjoy and I drove into the carrots. Our partners played excellent shots from the drop area, leaving putts of about ten feet for birdie. I was slightly away and stroked a putt that stopped just short of the cup.

Cloverjoy, seeing my putt come up short, rolled his putt some two and a half feet beyond the cup. Our short putt was conceded, but we decided to have the doctor putt the two-and-a-half-footer.

He stared at us for several seconds before lining up the putt, and then he stepped away. He lined up the putt again and tapped it slightly, and the ball stopped on the edge of the hole. He waited about a minute before picking up his ball. The match was now even.

We halved the seventh and eighth holes and moved on to the par-5 ninth.

Miss O'Toole still had the honors. She smacked a drive of some 240 yards that drifted into a fairway bunker to the left.

The doctor stood on the tee for several seconds and stared down the fairway. He then teed up his ball and blasted a drive of at least 280 yards down the fairway.

Walking to our ball, I told Miss O'Toole that I wasn't going to try anything heroic from the bunker. I just wanted to explode it out far enough to give her a shot at the green with her 3-wood. I entered the bunker and saw my ball was about three feet from the side. An 8-iron should get me out and advance the ball far enough to give Miss O'Toole a 3-wood shot that would give me a short iron to the green. I took several practice strokes before digging my feet in the sand and then swung. The ball hit the lip of the bunker and advanced no more than ten yards in the rough. I felt sick.

Miss O'Toole told me not to fret because she had a good lie and could power her 3-wood down the fairway, close enough to the green to give us a chance at par. She took several practice swings before lining up her shot and blasting the ball down the fairway about 220 yards. That would give me a short iron shot to the green for our fourth shot.

Meanwhile, Cloverjoy was standing over his partner's drive with his 3-wood in hand. The doctor stood aside, and Cloverjoy took several practice swings and then hit a shot that landed about twenty yards from the green.

I realized we would be lucky to par this hole. I approached our ball and decided to use my 6-iron, which should have been more than enough club to reach the green. Perhaps because of pent-up anger from my poor bunker shot, I struck a shot that landed on the back edge of the green and trickled off. Miss O'Toole would have to sink a chip shot for par.

Meanwhile, the doctor was addressing his short pitch shot. He lofted a shot that landed about ten feet from the flagstick and rolled another five feet, giving them an excellent shot at a birdie. Miss O'Toole was away, and she chipped to about six feet from the hole. We were still away, and I rolled our bogie putt past the hole. We looked briefly at our opponents' putt before conceding the hole. We were 1-down again.

I saw Dick by the tenth tee. He noted that we had lost the previous hole, and I told him we were 1-down. He reminded me that we had the back nine to play and were still very much in the match. I thanked him for his encouragement and told him we would be optimistic about our chances.

Miss O'Toole and her father walked over and said we should have some refreshment and rest. Soufflé was approaching with the food cart.

Both teams rested by the tenth tee. Cheese sandwiches and apple juice were our choice. Cloverjoy took two muffins and lemon soda, and the doctor had his usual beer and a sausage sandwich.

After about fifteen minutes, Sir Harold called us to the tenth tee.

The spectators were finishing their lunches and noisily surrounded the tee or moved down the fairway.

Cloverjoy was up, and I noted the breeze had gained strength and assumed he and the doctor were aware of this. He took two vigorous practice strokes and then belted a long slice into the bunker along the fairway.

As I stood on the tee, I felt confident that Miss O'Toole and I would regain the lead on this nine. I took several practice swings to loosen up, addressed the ball, and hit a low hook that landed in the lentil patch. Someone applauded—probably one of the doctor's fans.

Mary quickly found the ball, dropped it in the designated area, and had no trouble hitting an 8-iron to the green.

The doctor, in the bunker, then struck an 8-iron that landed on the back of the green and rolled into the bunker behind the green. I could sense a challenging bunker shot coming up.

Cloverjoy entered the bunker and saw he had a good lie. He dug his shoes into the sand and then blasted a shot that landed on the green, rolling to about five feet from the flag.

Miss O'Toole had a fifteen-foot putt for a birdie. She stroked a good putt that just missed the right edge of the hole.

The doctor spent little time surveying his five-footer before he lined up the putt and sank it for par.

Mary lined up her putt and stroked a putt that rolled into the cup. We saved par, which brought polite applause from the gallery.

The 212-yard eleventh hole was halved with bogies. The doctor and Mary were short on their tee shots, and Cloverjoy and I hit poor chip shots, leaving long par putts that our partners missed. The twelfth and thirteenth holes were halved with par.

For the par-5 fourteenth hole, we would be playing into the wind. Cloverjoy was up. The doctor muttered something to him, and he switched from his driver to a 3-wood.

Miss O'Toole and I looked at each other and wondered what they were thinking. I suspected the doctor didn't want Cloverjoy to slice into the mustard. The drop zone was at the base of the growth, lengthening the distance to the hole by some thirty yards.

Cloverjoy aimed left and hit a drive that started left, but it drifted back to the fairway.

I stepped to the tee, aimed left, and smacked a drive that landed at the edge of the rough—well beyond Cloverjoy's drive.

The doctor hammered his shot down the fairway some 240 yards, leaving them with a short iron to the green.

Miss O'Toole struck a 3-wood down the fairway, leaving me with a wedge to the green.

Cloverjoy's approach shot to the green hung up in the breeze and came up short.

I hit my wedge about twenty feet from the flagstick.

The doctor followed by chipping five feet beyond the flag, leaving Cloverjoy with a delicate downhill putt.

On the green, Miss O'Toole lined up the twenty-footer and stroked it by the right lip of the cup. The tap-in was conceded.

Cloverjoy and the doctor surveyed the five-footer, and the doctor pointed to where Cloverjoy should aim. As soon as he struck it, I could see it was going to miss on the low side of the hole. We had won the hole, and the match was even.

The par-3 fifteenth hole was halved with par. The hole played downwind, and Miss O'Toole and the doctor hit 6-irons to the green. I missed a fifteen-foot birdie putt, and Cloverjoy left a twelve-footer several inches short. The remaining putts were conceded, and the match remained even.

Sixteen was a 400-yard par-4 playing downwind. From the tee, I looked out at the potato patch on the right and the pot bunker along the left side of the fairway. If I was going to miss the fairway, driving into the potatoes was safer. After two lazy practice swings, I struck a drive down the middle about 230 yards.

Cloverjoy stepped to the tee, and the doctor pointed out that the potatoes were a safer play. Cloverjoy smacked a drive that the wind carried some 260 yards down the right side of the fairway.

My drive had left Miss O'Toole with a midiron to the green, and her shot landed about ten feet from the flagstick.

The doctor sized up his shot and used a short-iron. His ball landed about six feet from the flagstick. Our partners' shots left us with birdie putts that Cloverjoy and I missed. A birdie would have given us a one-hole advantage and made the next hole less daunting.

The 440-yard seventeenth hole was slight dogleg left, and we were now playing into the wind. A large bunker and a growth of spinach lay along the left side of the fairway. A large bunker guarded the green on the right.

Miss O'Toole went to the tee and hammered a drive of about 230 yards along the right side of the fairway.

The doctor smacked a drive of some 260 yards that just missed the spinach.

Walking to my partner's drive, I could see there was no way I was going to hit the green. My 5-wood would carry about two hundred yards against the wind. I aimed down the left side of the fairway to avoid the bunker to the right of the green. My 5-wood missed the bunker, but it left us at least twenty yards short of the green.

Cloverjoy was ready to play a 3-iron. His shot appeared to be on a line to the green, but the wind drifted the ball into the bunker.

The next shot was Miss O'Toole's. She played a pitch shot that landed about eight feet from the flag.

The doctor would play from the bunker. He blasted the ball out to about five feet from the flag.

Cloverjoy and I had par putts that we both missed, and I noticed the gallery was walking toward the eighteenth green.

Finally, we came to the eighteenth hole all tied. Eighteen was a 565-yard par-5 dogleg right, and we had the wind at our backs. A dozen or so onlookers stood around the tee.

I felt quite nervous as I stared down the fairway from the tee.

Miss O'Toole came up to me and, "Swing hard—the tomatoes are no problem."

I thought, *What she really means is that I probably can't reach the tomatoes with my drive.* She was right. My drive stopped just short of the tomato growth on the right. Cloverjoy's drive was just beyond mine.

When we reached my drive, Miss O'Toole's father handed her the 3-wood. "Give it all you've got."

Miss O'Toole belted a shot that landed about sixty yards short of the green.

The doctor lined up his 3-wood and hammed a beautiful wind-aided shot that landed just short of the green and rolled to about twenty feet from the flag. I could hear the applause from the spectators around the green and sensed they might make an eagle.

I stood behind my ball, wedge in hand, and realized I had to hit the ball close enough to the flag that a birdie was possible. Mary reminded me the wind was behind me. "Don't overshoot the green." I took several practice swings and then addressed the ball. I swung and saw the ball fly in line with the flagstick. It landed maybe two feet from the hole, hitting the flagstick and rolling about ten feet away. Cheers and applause followed.

On the green, Cloverjoy lined up an eagle putt. He and the doctor lined it up, and then Cloverjoy rolled a good putt that stopped about a foot short of the hole. Rather than concede their putt at this time, our opponents marked their ball.

Miss O'Toole had to make the ten-footer to ensure a birdie and remain in a tie. She and her father surveyed the putt before she took her stance. After two practice swings, she rolled a putt that I thought would surely drop, but it spun around the hole and stayed on the lip. We waited several agonizing seconds to see if it would fall before the doctor came forward and said it was good. We conceded their putt, and applause followed.

Mary had tears in her eyes as we walked over to congratulate our opponents.

The doctor praised her and said she was as tough an opponent as he had faced in previous tournaments here.

I hugged Mary and told her I was sorry I didn't play better and wished she could be my partner if I played here next year.

Mary's friends rushed over to her as we all stood on the green.

Sir Harold made his way to where the two teams were standing and gave Mary a big hug before congratulating Cloverjoy and Dr. Middlefield. He told us to follow him to the clubhouse.

Mary and I and the winners followed the jeep back to the clubhouse, and Soufflé opened the champagne bottles.

Leffingwell and Grafton attempted to keep the spectators out, but some pushed their way in.

Cloverjoy appeared overwhelmed by the crowd. Some of them were congratulating him, and others were praising their "Mary." I joined Dick, and after a glass of champagne, we decided to take the bus back to the Prince Rupert. We were both invited to Excelsior House later that evening as former winners.

Dinner at Excelsior House evolved into a rather raucous affair. After Sir Harold's toast to the winners and the runners-up, Mr. O'Toole toasted his host, the winners, the former winners, and a few close relatives of the O'Toole family who had been invited. It was all amusing at first, but then it became a bit annoying. Fortunately, once dinner was served, the evening settled down.

I excused myself early because I wanted to write up my notes on today's play and pack for my trip to London tomorrow. I would catch a plane to return home and get ready for our PGA tournament in Minneapolis. Sir Harold would be expecting my report.

EPILOGUE

He had reached the stage when his handicap was a wobbly
twelve and, as you are no doubt aware, it is then that a man
really begins to golf in the true sense of the word.
—P. G. Wodehouse

Golf is the best game in the world at which to be bad.
—A. A. Milne

I hadn't planned to attend the Open this year. Few American golfers
were interested in playing there, and my editor felt my efforts should be
directed at baseball. However, when Arnold Palmer announced he was
going to play in the Centenary Open at St. Andrews, my plans and that
of my editor changed. Palmer hoped to duplicate Ben Hogan's winning
the Masters, US Open, and British Open in the same year. So far, Palmer
had won the Masters and the recent US Open, storming back from seven
shots down during the final round. The sports world was focused on his
upcoming quest for the British Open.

I had informed Sir Harold several months ago that I would not be
competing at Gnomewood, and at that time, I would not be reporting
on the Open. Sir Harold was aware the American golf professionals were
reluctant to travel across the pond because the prize money didn't cover
the cost of the trip, but in the back of my mind, I toyed with the idea that
I might visit Gnomewood during its own tournament.

With the Open in mind, I notified our travel office that I needed a
flight to Scotland and a hotel room at St. Andrews. I planned to arrive on
July 1 to cover the qualifying rounds played on both the old course and

the new course. I informed Dick that I would be attending the Open and was looking forward to seeing him there.

Upon arriving at St. Andrews, I contacted Dick at the Old Course Hotel. I was staying at a small hotel near the University of St. Andrews. We met at his hotel and enjoyed a beer, and I told him I wasn't playing at Gnomewood this year—but I hoped to get there sometime after the Open was completed. After catching up on what we had been reporting so far this year, we walked to the practice range to watch the players warming up for tomorrow's first qualifying round. I saw Palmer on the range; he stood out with his smooth, powerful swing. Another golfer who caught my eye was a young South African, Gary Player. He was hitting crisp, accurate iron shots. Another golfer of note on the range was Dick Metz, a winner on our PGA tour.

After two qualifying rounds, Gary Player led with a score of 135. Palmer easily qualified, but Metz failed to qualify. The next day, the tournament began. Kel Nagel, from Australia, forged ahead, and after three rounds, he was leading Palmer by four strokes. On the final day, Palmer—with his typical flair for the dramatic—birdied four holes on the back nine, but he fell one stroke short of Nagle, who won with a score of 278 to Palmer's 279. In an interview after the tournament ended, Palmer expressed his desire to return to the Open next year. He had come so close to winning.

I stayed in Scotland a few more days to play Carnoustie before traveling south to Gnomewood-by-Sea.

Upon arriving at the Gnomewood Links unannounced, the first person I met was Leffingwell, and he was delighted to see me. I said I was there as an observer this year. I hadn't made a hotel reservation, but Leffingwell was sure I could get a room at the Prince Rupert. With Sir Harold's help, I did get a room with a toilet and a rudimentary shower. Sir Harold was glad I could make the trip to Gnomewood to watch the competition and meet the players, most of whom I had gotten to know the previous three tournaments.

The links appeared to be in excellent condition. Apparently, there had been enough rain to stimulate the fairways to a lustrous green glow. I had missed the qualifying round and the first day of match play. Looking at the day's competition, I noted neither the doctor nor Si Bumly were listed. Bumly had failed to qualify, and the doctor was rumored to be visiting a spa in Switzerland—probably to "dry out."

Miss Emma Littlefield, a schoolteacher from the St. Albans area, was partnered with Geoff Cloverjoy. She had qualified for the Ladies Open last year. Miss Shotwell was attending university and had reduced her playing schedule, and Miss O'Toole was playing in a tournament in Wales.

As the tournament progressed, the team of David Knibbles and Harlow Houndstooth faced Winston Peebles and Cyril Popinjay in the final match. The teams were tied after eighteen holes and required two extra holes before Peebles and Popinjay birdied the second extra hole to win.

Walking back to the clubhouse after the final match, I met Dick—who also had just returned from the Open—and he asked if I was planning to attend the Open at Royal Birkdale next year. He was also impressed by Palmer's emphatic desire to play in next year's Open. I said I hoped to, depending on what sporting events I was expected to cover back home. I added that I didn't think I would attend the Ryder Cup matches later this year at Royal Lytham & St. Annes, because I was sure I would be expected to cover college football at the same time.

Dick speculated that if Palmer maintained his current level of success, there would be considerable interest in the Open among American golf professionals and golf fans following his career.

I didn't attend the winner's banquet at Excelsior House even though—as a former winner—I was invited. I had checked out of the Prince Rupert and took the late train back to London. The next day, I flew back to New York. Barbara and Susan were delighted to see me. I had brought them sweaters from Scotland, which they greatly appreciated.

As I finished unpacking, I reflected on how lucky I had been to have Dick as a friend and to have played at Gnomewood and won with Miss Shotwell as a partner. My golf game had never been better. A poem by the late sportswriter Grantland Rice came to mind:

> Dame Fortune is a cockeyed wench,
> As someone's said before,
> And yet the old dame plays her part
> In any winning score.
> Take all the credit you deserve,
> heads up in winning pride.
> But don't forget that Lady Luck
> was riding on your side.
> —Grantland Rice, *The Tumult and the Shouting*, 1954

APPENDIX
(REVISIONS OF GNOMEWOOD LINKS, 1960)

The following changes were made in hopes that Gnomewood might be chosen as a site for qualifying for the Open or the British Amateur.

Hole 1. Artichoke. The hole is now 420 yards and descends slightly to an elevated green. A bunker lies about 230 yards from the tee, on the right, and another bunker guards the right side of the green. A growth of artichokes lies along the fairway on the right for about one hundred yards. The left side of the fairway is about fifty yards from a utility road that runs parallel to the fairway.

Hole 2. Asparagus. The hole remains at 385 yards, with a slight dogleg to the right. The green slants from right to left and is guarded by single bunkers right and left. An asparagus patch lies about fifty yards from the green on the right.

Hole 3. Beet. The hole is now a par-5 dogleg left of 515 yards. A drive along the left side of the fairway should allow the better player to go for the green with a long iron. However, a large fairway bunker lies beside the fairway where it bends left, and another bunker lies behind the green. A bunker was added to guard the right side of the green. A small beet patch lies behind the green, in the rough.

Hole 4. Broccoli. The hole remains a par-3 of 165 yards. Bunkers guard the green on the right, left, and behind. A broccoli plot lies along the fairway, on the left, and is surrounded by deep rough.

Hole 5. Cabbage. The hole is now four hundred yards. Cabbage flanks the fairway on the right for about thirty yards. The green is relatively small and is elevated in the middle, which tends to repel shots.

Hole 6. Carrot. The hole remains a 410-yard dogleg left. There is a growth of elephant grass in the rough about 250 yards from the tee, where the fairway bends left, and a growth of carrots is on the right. Most players will aim right to avoid the elephant grass, and if their drive lands in the carrots, they take a drop outside the carrots in short rough. Two pot bunkers guard the green on the right.

Hole 7. Celery. The hole remains a 430-yard dogleg left. There is a growth of celery on the left where the fairway bends. The generous-sized green is guarded by pot bunkers right and left.

Hole 8. Cucumber. This is now a 162-yard par-3 and plays to an elevated green. A cucumber patch lies along the green on the left, and a large bunker guards the green on the right.

Hole 9. Eggplant. The hole remains a 525-yard par-5. A growth of eggplants flanks the right fairway about two hundred yards from the tee for about twenty yards. Two bunkers lie along the fairway in the rough on the left about 250 yards from the tee. The green is guarded by two pot bunkers on the right and is the farthest point from the clubhouse.

Since the back nine lies relatively close to the ocean, the prevailing wind will affect the ball more than on the front nine.

Hole 10. Lentil. The hole is now a 414-yard dogleg right, usually playing downwind. A bunker lies where the fairway bends right. A growth of lentils lies along the fairway from the bunker extending to the right side of the green. A large bunker lies behind the green. A drive that lands at the bend in the fairway allows for a 7-iron or 8-iron to the green.

Hole 11. Lettuce. This hole remains a 212-yard par-3, playing into the wind. Two pot bunkers guard the green on the left. A growth of lettuce lies alongside the fairway on the right. The hole requires a well-hit long iron to reach the green.

Hole 12. Parsley. This is now a par-4 of 395 yards, playing downwind. A large bunker lies in front of and to the right of the green, and a pot bunker lies left of the green. Parsley lies on both sides of the fairway.

Hole 13. Onion. This hole remains a 145-yard par-3 plays to a slightly elevated green, behind which is a large, deep bunker created by a German bomb in 1940. A smaller bunker guards the green on the right. An onion patch lies along the fairway on the right. Because the hole usually plays downwind, there is a tendency to overshoot the green and land in the deep bunker behind the green.

Hole 14. Mustard. No change. The hole is a 517-yard par-5, playing into the wind. Two bunkers lie beside the fairway on the left, and a third bunker lies in front of the green. A growth of mustard parallels the fairway on both sides. Only the longest hitters can reach the green in two shots.

Hole 15. Pea. The hole is a 185-yard par-3, playing downwind. A pot bunker lies on either side of the green, and a third bunker lies behind the green. A large pea patch lies along the left side of the fairway.

Hole 16. Potato. The hole is now 430 yards, playing downwind. A growth of potatoes lies along the fairway on the right, in the middle of which is a bunker. Behind the green is a large bunker, the result of another German bomb. The somewhat Y-shaped green offers three possible flagstick positions.

Hole 17. Spinach. The hole remains a 440-yard par-4 dogleg left, playing into the prevailing breeze. A bunker guards the front-left side of the green. The growth of spinach begins about two hundred yards from the tee and extends just short of the green.

Hole 18. Tomato. The hole remains a 565-yard par-5 dogleg right, playing downwind. A bunker lies in the rough about 250 yards from the tee where the fairway bends right. Two bunkers lie on either side of the green, and a large bunker has been added behind the green. A large growth of tomatoes lies along the left side of the fairway. The prevailing wind off the ocean will tempt the player to go for the green in two strokes.

Total yardage: 6,710

Printed in the United States
by Baker & Taylor Publisher Services

Printed in the United States
by Baker & Taylor Publisher Services